PENGUIN ENGl

ONE HUNDRED USEFUL
EXERCISES IN ENGLISH

By the same author

Published by Longman
The Use of Tenses in English
Peculiarities in English Grammar
British & American English, Books One & Two
New Intermediate English Course
    Students' Books One & Two
    Teachers' Books One & Two
Practice in the Use of English
Proficiency in the Use of English
Practice in Structure & Usage, Books One & Two
The New Intermediate English Grammar

Published by Nelson
English Proficiency through Practice

Published by Bell & Hyman
O Level English Practice

100
ONE HUNDRED USEFUL EXERCISES IN ENGLISH

WITH ANSWERS

JOHN MILLINGTON WARD

PENGUIN ENGLISH

For permission to reproduce copyright material, the publishers
gratefully acknowledge the following: the University of London School Examinations Board
for exercises 21 and 49; Adolf K. Placzek for the excerpt from *Mrs Miniver* by
Jan Struther in exercise 71; Times Newspapers Limited for the Fourth
Leader that appeared in *The Times* on 14 November 1958,
reproduced here in exercise 95.

PENGUIN BOOKS

Published by the Penguin Group
Penguin Books Ltd, 27 Wrights Lane, London W8 5TZ, England
Penguin Putnam Inc., 375 Hudson Street, New York, New York 10014, USA
Penguin Books Australia Ltd, Ringwood, Victoria, Australia
Penguin Books Canada Ltd, 10 Alcorn Avenue, Toronto, Ontario, Canada M4V 3B2
Penguin Books (NZ) Ltd, 182–190 Wairau Road, Auckland 10, New Zealand

Penguin Books Ltd, Registered Offices: Harmondsworth, Middlesex, England

First published 1987
5 7 9 10 8 6

Copyright © John Millington Ward 1987
All rights reserved

Filmset in 11½/13 Plantin

Printed in England by Clays Ltd, St Ives plc

Except in the United States of America, this book is sold subject
to the condition that it shall not, by way of trade or otherwise, be lent,
re-sold, hired out, or otherwise circulated without the publisher's
prior consent in any form of binding or cover other than that in
which it is published and without a similar condition including this
condition being imposed on the subsequent purchaser

CONTENTS

The Exercises	9–144
Key to the Exercises	145–201
Index	202–203

This book provides wide-range and comprehensive practice in English Usage, Rephrasing, Comprehension, Appreciation, Grammar, etc. It also offers practice in many of the particular skills that Candidates for various examinations will require, notably the First Certificate of the University of Cambridge.

THE 100 EXERCISES

THE EXERCISES

1 Imagine that you are listening to Mr Blake talking on the telephone to a Mrs Lewis. You cannot, of course, hear what Mrs Lewis says but you might be able to guess. Write your guesses in the empty spaces.

    Mr Blake: May I speak to Mr Levis, please?

1 Mrs Lewis:
   Mr Blake: Lewis? Oh, I'm sorry. I must have written it down wrongly. Well, good morning. Mrs Lewis. Is your husband at home?

2 Mrs Lewis:
   Mr Blake: What time will he be getting up, please?

3 Mrs Lewis:
   Mr Blake: Oh, do forgive me! I'm awfully sorry to hear that. I thought you said he was *still* in bed. The line isn't very clear. Well, Mrs Lewis, my name is Blake and I'm ringing from ...

4 Mrs Lewis:
   Mr Blake: No, I've never had the pleasure of meeting him.

5 Mrs Lewis:
   Mr Blake: I don't know it, of course. It's just a way of speaking.

6 Mrs Lewis:
　Mr Blake: I'll tell you what I want in just a moment, Mrs Lewis. First, though, may I introduce myself? As I said, my name is Blake and I'm ringing from ...

7 Mrs Lewis:
　Mr Blake: Nobody gave me your number.

8 Mrs Lewis:
　Mr Blake: From the telephone book. Every day I take a dozen or so names from the telephone book and ...

9 Mrs Lewis:
　Mr Blake: I'll tell you in a second. But let me start at the beginning again. I'm ringing from the circulation department of the *Daily Echo* to say ...

10 Mrs Lewis:
　Mr Blake: A newspaper, dear lady. A famous newspaper.

11 Mrs Lewis:
　Mr Blake: Oh, I beg your pardon. The circulation department. That's the one that looks after the sales of a newspaper.

12 Mrs Lewis:
　Mr Blake: Oh, it might well concern you, Mrs Lewis. We can now deliver the *Daily Echo* to your house at 5 o'clock every morning.

13 Mrs Lewis:
　Mr Blake: You don't have to get up at 5 o'clock. We just deliver it at that time. We put it in your letter-box.

14 Mrs Lewis:
　Mr Blake: Really? I thought everybody had one these days. In that case we can leave it on your doorstep.

15 Mrs Lewis:
　Mr Blake: I don't think there's much danger of that, really. It's not as if it would be a bundle of pound notes on the doorstep.

16 Mrs Lewis:
   Mr Blake: Well, mainly perhaps to have the fullest possible picture of what is going on in the world.

17 Mrs Lewis:
   Mr Blake: But TV isn't really enough, is it? A newspaper is able to give so many more details than the TV news can.

18 Mrs Lewis:
   Mr Blake: With respect, Mrs Lewis, I think everybody ought to be interested in details these days. But anyway, apart from that side of the matter, our newspaper offers many other things to interest its readers.

19 Mrs Lewis:
   Mr Blake: Articles, features, cooking recipes, cinema programmes – to name just a few.

20 Mrs Lewis:
   Mr Blake: Nor do I, to tell you the truth. The films these days aren't as good as they used to be, but ... Hello? Mrs Lewis? Are you there? Hello? Good heavens, she's hung up! What a very unpleasant woman.

2 Fill each of the blank spaces with ONE of these verbs, in an appropriate form:

ask   speak   talk   say   tell   order

1 I don't know the hotel personally, but it is ………… to be quite a good one.

2 Sit down and ………… me exactly what happened.

3 Let's ………… the new neighbours to dinner next week.

4 We'd better ………… the whole thing over again before we make a decision.

5 The Minister is going to ………… in Parliament tomorrow about unemployment.

6 The doctor took his temperature and then ………… him straight to bed.

7 Some people ………… that the imported cola is better than the local product but I can't ………… the difference.

8 Daddy, Nigel has ………… me to marry him!

9 And what have you got to ………… for yourself, you wretched boy?

10 I have been ………… them that they are making a great mistake.

11 Yes, I think I ………… German well enough to make myself understood at least.

12 Waiter, we're ready to ………… now.

13 We were ………… to her last night and she didn't once ………… a word about her illness.

14 Go and ………… that man what he is doing here. He wasn't invited.

15 The miners here are ………… about going on strike again.

3 Fill the blank spaces in these sentences with the word that correctly describes the document or piece of paper appropriate to the situation.

EXAMPLE   Two months before he died, Jonathan made a new .... in which he left everything to me.
ANSWER   will

1 Peter didn't have enough cash to pay for his dinner so he made out a ....

2 You can't buy that medicine without a .... from a doctor.

3 I suppose he'll want to see the .... that will prove that I have really passed the examination.

4 Josephine wrote to her bank to ask for an up-to-date .... of her account.

5 I finished my book a few days ago. I'm sending the .... to the publisher tomorrow.

6 Our house is rather difficult to find. I'll draw you a little .... to show you the best way.

7 What a delicious pudding you've made! Could you please give me the ....?

8 The income tax inspector won't accept this expense unless you can give him an official ....

9 As the doctor came into the room the nurse handed him the temperature .... of the patient.

10 If you want the estate agent to sell the house for you, you'll have to let him see the .... that show you're the legal owner.

4 'I'm terribly sorry' expresses an apology, and 'Do please turn the lights on' expresses a request. Choose from the list below what is expressed by each of the following sentences.

ACCEPTANCE	INVITATION
ACCUSATION	OFFER
ADMISSION	PROTEST
COMPLAINT	REFUSAL
DENIAL	SUGGESTION

1 You might have telephoned me to say you were going to be late.
2 All right, let them stay if they want to so much.
3 I will *not* go there again.
4 What about going for a picnic tomorrow?
5 I didn't do it.
6 Won't you come in and have a drink?
7 You've used my toothbrush again.
8 This is the third time the car I bought from you has gone wrong.
9 I'm afraid I didn't tell you the exact truth about what happened.
10 Can I get you something to eat?

5 Finish each of the incomplete sentences below in such a way that it has the same meaning as the sentence above it.

EXAMPLE   It would be wise for us to take raincoats.
         We'd ....
ANSWER   We'd better take raincoats.

1 This suitcase is too small for all my things.
   This suitcase is not ....

2 Their house is so far away that we can't walk there.
   It is such ....

3 'Can you guess who has just left?' he asked us.
   He asked us if ....

4 The architect worked on the plans for six months.
   The architect spent ....

5 On the day she agreed to marry him, he was happier than he had ever been in his life.
   The day she agreed to marry him was ....

6 I haven't seen so much rain for a long time.
   It's ....

7 Malcolm was originally going to buy a car, but he bought a motor-cycle instead.
   Instead ....

8 Please explain this letter to me.
   Please tell me ....

9 You cannot go into that restaurant without a jacket and tie.
   Unless ....

10 It is high time for us to go home.
   It's time we ....

11 I can study properly only if I sit at a desk.
   Sitting at a desk is ....

12 Jennifer regretted her foolish behaviour.
   Jennifer wished ....

13 We took more clothes than we needed on holiday last summer.
   We needn't ....

14 Is it really necessary for me to arrive so early?
Do I ....

15 Someone has stolen the boss's car.
The boss has ....

16 Take an umbrella with you. It may rain this afternoon.
Take an umbrella in ....

17 We worked on the garden the whole weekend.
We spent ....

18 Two new suits are being made for him.
He is ....

19 Leonard felt sick because he was eating polluted shellfish.
If Leonard ....

20 The only thing I forgot to put in the picnic basket was the bottle-opener.
I remembered ....

6 The word in capital letters at the end of each of these sentences can be changed in such a way that it forms a word that fits suitably in the blank space. Fill each blank space in this way.

EXAMPLE The bloodstain on her dress was very ....
NOTICE

ANSWER The bloodstain on her dress was very *noticeable*.

1 Nobody wanted to live in the .... part of the town. INDUSTRY

2 The police asked him to give a .... of the suitcase he had lost. DESCRIBE

3 He had no .... that he was being watched. SUSPECT

4 This is Alexandra, my personal .... ASSIST

5 Although some of my work-mates quickly found new jobs after the factory closed down, my brother and I were .... for several months. EMPLOY

6 Although I was positive that the girl had stolen my ring, I could not find any .... PROVE

7 The doctor dealt with the hysterical patient with ....
UNDERSTAND

8   There's a .... at the British Embassy tonight.   RECEIVE

9   The next-door neighbours are so .... that we have stopped trying to talk to them.   FRIEND

10 Yes, I can speak a little Spanish because I spent some of my .... in Spain.   BOY

11 This jewel is not simply valuable, it is ....   VALUE

12 Susan has two bad characteristics: jealousy and ....   POSSESS

13 After all he has done for us, it would be very .... of us if we didn't do this for him now.   HELP

14 With the world's population increasing at the present rate, by the year 2000 it is feared there will be a terrible food ....   SHORT

15 Penelope has .... failed her driving test again.   FORTUNE

16 Fruit is always .... in summer here.   PLENTY

17 The .... of the money from the cash-box shows that somebody in this office is a thief.   APPEAR

18 You must accept the .... of the committee.   DECIDE

19 Vernon and Wanda arrived late at the opera and were refused .... until the end of the first act.   ADMIT

20 This coat is too short for today. Do you think you could .... it a little for me?   LONG

7 Make all the changes and additions necessary to produce, from the following ten groups of words and phrases, a complete letter from Anne to her Aunt Edwina.

Examine this example carefully to see what kind of changes and additions need to be made.

Norman / wish / he / be able / take / girlfriend / dinner / last night / as well / theatre / but not have / money / both

Norman wished he had been able to take his girlfriend out to dinner last night as well as to the theatre but he did not have enough money for both.

Dear Aunt Edwina,

    Thank / very much / present / just / arrive

1 ....

    What / lovely dress / suit me / wonderfully / be / most grateful

2 ....

    Jack and I / go / Covent Garden / celebrate / this evening

3 ....

    Placido Domingo / sing / *Don Giovanni* / von Karajan / conduct

4 ....

    Afterwards / favourite restaurant / champagne / special occasion

5 ....

    Twenty-first birthday / great day / life / come once

6 ....

    Next great day / be / wedding / probably / Spring

7 ....

    In spite / you / live / far / we both / hope much / you / come

8 ....

    Easy / you / stay / with us / plenty / space / because / big house

9 ....

Tell / definite date / as soon / fixed
10 ....

With special love to you,

Anne

8 Fill each of the numbered blank spaces in this passage with ONE suitable word.

A light rain was .... 1 over the city of Salzburg. The lights of the shops twinkled in the gathering dusk. A church clock .... 2 the hour of six.

A young man walked slowly .... 3 the wet pavement. His raincoat collar was turned up .... 4 his ears. His hands were .... 5 deep into his pockets. He came to a stop for a .... 6 moments in .... 7 of each shop window and .... 8 its contents with a wholly false interest.

Two plain-clothes policemen, a hundred yards behind him strolled along the street .... 9 making any pretence .... 10 studying the shop windows. There was no need for pretence because they knew that the young man knew he was .... 11 followed. When he stopped at a shop window, they simply slowed .... 12 their walk or came to a relaxed halt until he moved on.

The young man stopped a little longer outside the bookshop. The policemen came to a halt .... 13. One of them took a packet of cigarettes from his pocket and offered it to his .... 14. The young man watched them out of the .... 15 of his eye. He saw their heads .... 16 as they lit their cigarettes under the rain. He turned and walked quickly into the Zipfer Bierhaus next door.

The policemen saw him .... 17 as they straightened their heads. They threw down their cigarettes and began to run. They ran lightly, swiftly, ... 18 athletes. In almost no .... 19 at all they reached the entrance of the bierhaus. 'It's all right,' said the senior, stopping and looking up at the sign over the door. 'What .... 20 in has to come out. We'll just wait for him.'

9 The omission of words like *each other*, *yourself*, *herself*, *ourselves* etc. sometimes changes the meaning of a sentence and sometimes it does not. Look at these ten sentences and say in which of them the omission of the words in *italics* would change the meaning.

EXAMPLE　　The children were dressing *each other*.
ANSWER　　Omission would change the meaning.

EXAMPLE　　Keep *yourself* as warm as possible.
ANSWER　　Omission would not change the meaning.

1. My wife and I met *each other* on a ship going to Japan.
2. She has given *herself* till Christmas for the work to be finished.
3. The old lady drew *herself* back in disgust.
4. We are preparing *ourselves* for the final examination.
5. Van and Eva helped *each other* to prepare the meal.
6. Have you ever shaved *yourself* with an open razor?
7. The two women kissed *each other* with false warmth.
8. The wolves approached *each other*, snarling ferociously.
9. Bill, do stop showing off like that! Behave *yourself* for once.
10. The girls happily showed *each other* their new dresses.

10 Here are twenty short dialogues. In each case, ONE word in the second speaker's reply would be spoken with some emphasis. Can you say which word it is?

EXAMPLE Molly: I've eaten far too much again.
               Diana: I'm afraid we all have.
ANSWER   Diana: I'm afraid we *ALL* have.

1 Bernard: I hear he'd just got out of the bath when his roof blew away.
   Anthony: No, he was just getting in the bath when the roof blew away.

2 Pauline: She doesn't really want this, does she?
   Phyllis: You'd better go and ask her.

3 James: You've got some lipstick on your cheek.
   Roger: Let me look. My God, so I have!

4 Doreen: The bathroom still occupied! Who on earth is taking so long?
   Cicely: Who always takes so long?

5 Donald: Was your hotel comfortable?
   Philip: Well, I can't say it was actually uncomfortable.

6 Valerie: You haven't made the beds yet.
   Winifred: Stop fussing! I'm going to make them.

7 Andrew: What a pretty woman his wife is!
   Robert: That's not his wife. It's their new cleaning woman.

8 Eileen: We didn't understand much of his lecture last night.
   Louise: I think very few people understood it.

9 Gordon: I can't find my glasses again.
   Marina: You ought to attach a chain to them.

10 Alison: They're going to sell their car.
   Godfrey: That lovely Rolls! It must be breaking their hearts.

11 Vincent: This brand of vodka has become very expensive nowadays.
   Edward: It's not the cost of it that worries me.

12 George: I love you very much, my sweet.
   Brenda: I love you very much, my honeybear.

13 Edith: Did they get away yesterday?
    Carol: No, they're leaving this morning.

14 Larry: Could you lend me a pencil?
    Bruce: Sorry, I haven't got one.

15 Lilian: Isn't Mummy ever going to get supper ready?
    Maisie: I think she's waiting for one of us to get it ready.

16 Joyce: Why didn't you bring home a loaf of bread, as I especially asked you?
    Eddie: I especially did bring home a loaf of bread.

17 Graham: I can't see my umbrella among all these others.
    Patrick: Nor can I. But here is my hat, at least.

18 Sophia: I was at school with Maria Callas.
    Thalia: Good heavens! Do you mean the Callas?

19 Dudley: Father's agreed to let me have the car for the weekend.
    Michael: You're lucky. He wouldn't do that for anyone else.

20 Janet: Why did you tell them not to go to Washington in summer?
    Linda: Because it gets so humid that it's like a Turkish bath in summer.

11 Here are twenty sentences each with a blank space. Below each sentence are four words or phrases. Choose the one of these that most suitably fills the blank space.

1 Be careful! Here's a wasps' nest. Don't .... it.
   interfere   disturb   blast   thrill

2 No, it's no good. I've .... my time in trying to make it work.
   spent   spoiled   consumed   wasted

3 Our car is a much older .... than yours.
   model   pattern   manufacture   form

4 Because of the poor harvest, wheat prices have .... in the last six months.
   grown up   gone up   jumped up   sprung up

5 We'd better hurry. There's a .... to Uncle Timothy's patience.
top   bottom   border   limit

6 You thought I did wrong but the results .... my action.
agree   prove   approve   justify

7 I was very .... of myself for forgetting Mother's birthday.
disgraced   ashamed   shy   shocked

8 It usually takes a little while to .... in a new flat.
settle up   settle on   settle down   settle through

9 Didn't it ever .... to them that they would be punished?
occur   happen   enter   strike

10 You're very quiet today. What have you got on your ....?
attention   mind   spirit   mood

11 It's most unwise to .... in a quarrel between a man and his wife.
involve   poke   mix   interfere

12 To make a good omelette, you must .... the eggs very well.
beat   knock   thrash   bang

13 I can't see any easy .... to this rather complicated problem.
result   solution   reason   release

14 The civil servant .... his post because he disagreed with the Minister.
gave in   gave out   gave off   gave up

15 Madeleine struggled for a long time before she finally .... to free herself.
managed   succeeded   achieved   enabled

16 I'll let you have it back next Monday without ....
doubt   fail   miss   neglect

17 I don't .... to get married because I like being a bachelor.
risk   persist   intend   insist

18 Everybody is very anxious about the .... of the negotiations.
    outbreak   outcome   output   outlook

19 Do you really believe in the .... of the evil eye?
    being   occurrence   existence   realism

20 That fellow has a dishonest .... in his character.
    stripe   streak   stroke   strip

12 In the following ten sentences some phrases or words are printed in *italics*. Each of these can be replaced by one of the more informal phrases given below. Fill the brackets under each sentence with the phrase which you think best replaces the words in *italics*.

off hand	second hand	in hand
out of hand	on hand	to hand
had a hand	by hand	hand to hand
lend a hand	underhand	at hand
upper hand	hand in hand	on all hands

1 The letter from the President was passed from *one person to another* and read by everybody.
   (..)

2 We found a taxi very quickly and so we arrived at the station with about a quarter of an hour *to spare*.
   (..)

3 The police were suspicious; it appeared that more than one person had *taken part* in the robbery although no one else had been seen near the bank that night.
   (..)

4 We are rather lucky; we have all the necessary shops close *to where we live*.
   (..)

5 The businessman, knowing that he could not get the better of his competitors fairly, decided to use *unfair* methods to gain the advantage.
   (..)

6 You must be very careful when you buy a car that is *not new*.
(..)

7 With an inefficient teacher, even a good class can get quickly *into a state of disorder*.
(..)

8 Because the postal service was not at all reliable, we asked if the papers could be delivered *personally*.
(..)

9 I have heard that same rumour repeated *by many different sorts of people*.
(..)

10 There was so much disorder in the village after the flood that everybody had to *help* in putting things straight.
(..)

13 In each of these groups, two words have the same pronunciation. Which are they?

1	peace	3	pose	5	saw	7	shoot	9	toe
	peas		pause		sew		suit		too
	piece		paws		sore		chute		two
2	place	4	race	6	says	8	stairs	10	way
	plaice		raise		sees		stares		weigh
	plays		rays		seize		steers		why

14 Change the verbs in these sentences into their passive equivalents, and make whatever other changes are necessary.

Some will need only the simple, basic change:
EXAMPLE   They have given Bishop Tutu the Nobel Prize.
ANSWER   Bishop Tutu has been given the Nobel Prize.
    or   The Nobel Prize has been given to Bishop Tutu.

Others will need the more complicated construction that needs an infinitive:
EXAMPLE   The police allege that Simpson robbed three banks last year.
ANSWER   Simpson is alleged (by the police) to have robbed three banks last year.

NOTE   Avoid the impersonal construction with 'It' in this case: e.g. It is alleged (by the police) that Simpson robbed three banks last year.

1 Our postal service used to deliver parcels. Now we have to collect them.
2 The company says that the production figures have fallen short of expectations.
3 The police have given everyone two weeks to surrender any guns which they may possess illegally.
4 Many people believe that UFOs exist, never mind what the authorities say.
5 The Prime Minister is to visit the hospital tomorrow.
6 My family believes that this painting is worth a lot of money.
7 Didn't anyone tell you that we cannot allow people into the area unless they produce a certificate of inoculation?
8 The inquiry found that the riot had been started by anarchists.
9 Will they have to amputate his leg or will they save it?
10 The radio said last night that a volcano is erupting on the island of Xand.
11 The authorities are going to isolate the factory because of the atomic leak.

12 They say he was cleaning his pistol – and carelessness caused his death.

13 We need to go into that matter very carefully.

14 The newspaper reports that the survivors of the crash are on their way to hospital.

15 In my absence someone had broken the lock of my car and stolen the luggage on the back seat.

16 Please don't come to the station with me. I hate people saying goodbye to me through the window of a train.

17 Someone will have to pick up this broken glass or we mustn't allow the children to come anywhere near this room.

18 Evidence shows that Jackson was inside the house at the time of the murder.

19 Are you really going to allow me to drive your lovely Rolls-Royce?

20 They say the Princess is staying incognito at the Hilton.

15 Below are five groups of three words. Give one word which describes each group.

EXAMPLE coat, dress, trousers
ANSWER   clothes

1 table, chair, bed ....
2 car, bus, lorry ....
3 lunch, tea, supper ....
4 hammer, plane, saw ....
5 army, navy, airforce ....

Complete these sentences with one appropriate word concerning TRAVEL.

EXAMPLE The train .... from London to Glasgow lasts five hours.
ANSWER   journey

6 Yolanda likes to spend her holidays on a ship and last summer she went on a two-week luxury .... round the Mediterranean.
7 We were very glad to get off the aeroplane and stretch our legs after the fifteen-hour .... from Tokyo to London.
8 The large passenger ship, the *Titanic*, sank on its first .... in 1912.
9 A .... agent helps people to arrange their holidays.
10 Reginald will go on a business .... to Amsterdam tomorrow.

Give the name of the tool or implement that would be used for the job.

EXAMPLE Cutting down a tree
ANSWER   axe

11 Taking a cork out of a bottle ....
12 Putting a screw into wood ....
13 Digging a garden ....
14 Boiling water for tea ....
15 Making electricity ....

16 Fill each of these blank spaces with a suitable word or phrase of your choice.

EXAMPLE Two convicts are reported .... from the prison last night.
ANSWER   to have escaped *or* to have got away

1 It was not till .... dark glasses off that I realised she was a famous film star.
2 No sooner had the doctor gone to sleep than the telephone ....
3 If we had known you would have liked to come to our party, we .... invitation.

28

4 .... you move your car at once, you'll get a ticket.
5 I don't believe a word of what he says. He .... all up, I'm sure.
6 I saw a gun pointing at me. 'Don't make the slightest movement .... shoot!' said a voice softly.
7 The children were .... to their holiday.
8 Give .... tomorrow some time, will you? My number is 345-8899.
9 His mother went abroad last week, so it .... you saw at the theatre last night.
10 Richard would always prefer to drive himself .... by his wife.
11 It's your fault if you drop your glasses. You .... in that small pocket.
12 It was fine yesterday but it .... all day today, so I haven't finished the gardening.
13 You're looking very troubled. .... mind?
14 Roger would like .... Oxford, but he couldn't pass the entrance examination.
15 You say there aren't many taxis at night in this little town. I'm not surprised. I wouldn't have thought .... at all.
16 His wife has been examined by a dozen doctors but none of them .... her.
17 Don't forget to .... the lights before you come up to bed.
18 I asked in the shop if I could wash this material and they said it's better ....
19 If we hadn't found that taxi, we .... train.
20 I don't believe you're as strong as you say. .... see you lift that box.

17 Four phrases are printed after each of these short dialogues. Choose the one which will suitably fill the blank space

1 Sidney: Shall we stay at home or go for a walk?
   Margot: Which .... do yourself?

   A do you rather   C would you rather
   B will you rather   D did you rather

2 Becky: I didn't really enjoy the party last night.
   Adela: No, and ....

   A neither we did   C we didn't too
   B we didn't either   D so didn't we

3 Cecilia: I feel another dizzy spell coming on.
   Margery: I do wish .... get round to seeing a doctor.

   A you are going to   C you would
   B you will agree to   D you will

4 Mary: Would you give this note to Mr Tomlinson, please?
   Ross: Sorry, I can't. He ....

   A doesn't any more work here
   B any longer doesn't work here.
   C doesn't work any more here.
   D doesn't work here any longer.

5 Barbara: It's curious that Roy can't ski better.
   Leonora: I know. By the end of the month, he .... lessons for a full month.

   A will have   C has been having
   B will be having   D will have been having

6 Rex: It's already half-past six.
  Hal: Good heavens, so it is! It's time we ....

   A are gone   C were gone
   B are going   D shall go

7 Flora: You're awfully behind with the work, aren't you?
  Daisy: I know. I .... to the cinema last night.

   A oughn't to go   C haven't had to go
   B had not to go   D shouldn't have gone

8 Roland: Have the children had supper yet?
  Marion: No, and they're not used .... it so late.

   A to have   C to having
   B that they have   D of having

9 Hilda: Was the Minister's speech interesting?
  Miles: Yes, at first, but was .... long.

   A so much   C far too
   B too far   D too much

10 Grace: I wish your parents would invite us for a holiday.
   Monty: They can't. They have .... to accommodate
           us and the children too.

   A such a small house   C very small a house
   B a too small house   D too small a house

11 Hilary: I shan't be more than five or ten minutes now.
   Alfred: All right. I'll wait over there until .... ready.

   A you will be   C you were
   B you are   D you're going to be

12 Fay: The headmistress wants you in her study.
    Ivy: She's here already. I didn't think she .... till tomorrow.

    A will be coming   C is coming
    B was coming   D is to come

13 Deborah: When are they going to buy that house?
    Claudia: Didn't you know? They finally decided ....

    A not to be   C not
    B not to   D no

14 Alistair: I'm in an awful mess here. Could you give me a hand?
    Alexander: Certainly. What needs ....?

    A to be done   C to be doing
    B to do   D to have done

15 Irene: There were already five people in the car but they managed to squeeze me in.
    Larry: It .... a very comfortable journey.

    A can't be   C couldn't have been
    B mustn't have been   D couldn't be

16 Stewart: Let's go and have lunch.
    Herbert: I'll join you later. I mustn't stop .... on this for another ten minutes.

    A to be working   C to have worked
    B to work   D working

17 Joan: Could I have another spoonful of your delightful pudding?
    Maud: Oh dear, there doesn't seem to be ....

    A some left   C left any
    B any left   D leaving some

18 Lucian: I'm most grateful to you for getting the doctor in time.
    Miriam: If I hadn't, I think you ....

    A might have died   C would die
    B could die   D may have died

19 Freda: Do you know our city at all?
    Barry: No, it's the first time .... here.

    A I have been   C I had been
    B I was   D I am coming

20 Harvey: I think I'm well enough to get back to work.
    Gladys: Not really. You .... stay at home for another day or so.

    A should better   C would better
    B had better   D can better

33

18 Indicate clearly and fully, in any way that you wish, the difference in the meanings of the sentences in these pairs.

EXAMPLE a Nobody did anything that night.
b Nobody did nothing that night.

ANSWER a Everybody was lazy (or inactive) that night.
b Everybody was busy (or active) that night.

1 a Our car has been robbed!
b Our car has been stolen!

2 a Angela tried to push her car to start it, but couldn't manage it.
b Angela tried pushing her car to start it, but couldn't manage it.

3 a The climbers, who reached the top, had a wonderful view of the valley.
b The climbers who reached the top had a wonderful view of the valley.

4 a Good heavens, Pip! You must have your shoes polished.
b Good heavens, Pip! You must have polished your shoes.

5 a Maureen wondered, 'Which umbrella would go best with my new mackintosh?'
b Maureen wondered which umbrella would go best with my new mackintosh.

6 a They will arrive in time, I think.
b They will arrive on time, I think.

7 a The last thing the old man agreed to do was to make his will.
b Making his will was the last thing the old man would agree to do.

8 a It's warm enough to bathe today.
b It's too warm not to bathe today.

9 a Elizabeth is a princess, all right!
b All right, Elizabeth is a princess!

10 a We walked all that way to their house only to find whether they had left.
   b We walked all that way to their house only to find that they had left.

11 a This news of Adrian's is a bit worrying, isn't it?
   b This news of Adrian is a bit worrying, isn't it?

12 a The lemon trees, which were given some of that new fertiliser, produced very good fruit.
   b The lemon trees which were given some of that new fertiliser produced very good fruit.

13 a At yesterday's meeting, the two senior directors, Mr Blake and Mr Conway, voted against our proposal.
   b At yesterday's meeting, the two senior directors, Mr Blake and Mr Conway voted against our proposal.

14 a They treated him like a Head of State.
   b They treated him as a Head of State.

15 a I know Vanessa would like to have come to your party.
   b I know Vanessa would have liked to come to your party.

19 Fill each of the blank spaces in these sentences with ONE of the following particles.

DOWN   FOR   IN   OFF   OUT   UP

1 I've lost a lot of weight recently. I'll have to have my clothes taken ………

2 If William doesn't mend his ways, he'll end ……… in prison.

3 We don't often go to restaurants these days. It has become very expensive to eat ………

4 She got past the police at the gate by passing herself ……… as a doctor.

5 Our charwoman has just owned ……… that it was she who stole the jewel.

6 Another epidemic of cholera has just broken ……… in Lenghis.

7 Children, go into the garden and work ……… some of your energy there, not here in the house!

8 We're making ……… the village of Hayslope. Are we on the right road?

9 You have an awfully high temperature. I'm going to send ……… the doctor.

10 After living for years in a big house, we found it difficult to settle ……… in a flat.

11 Our car broke ……… on a lonely country road and we had to walk to the nearest village to get help.

12 I didn't quite take ……… what you said. Will you repeat it, please?

13 I'm ringing to ask if you could put me ……… for the night. All the hotels are full up.

14 It was a dull speech. My father dropped ……… in the middle of it, and we had to wake him when he began snoring.

15 Don't come to the station to see me ……… Let's say goodbye here.

16 I'm afraid you've missed your flight. It took .... ten minutes ago.

17 Peggy had a cold a few days ago but she's managed to throw it .... without having to go to bed.

18 I fell .... with the butcher today. He was very rude to me.

19 Randolph told me the whole lying story so convincingly that I was completely taken ...., at least at the beginning.

20 I picked .... the little I know of your language when I was here during the war.

20 Each word in the left-hand column below rhymes with one, and only one, word in the right-hand column. Can you say which rhymes with which?

1	bury	a	cheery
2	fiery	b	diary
3	glory	c	ferry
4	hairy	d	carry
5	marry	e	hurry
6	lorry	f	sorry
7	weary	g	story
8	worry	h	vary

21 Carefully read the following passage twice, and then answer the questions.

    Patch noticed Cristoforo studying the sky. It was already the vivid trembling azure of the travel posters, and against it the mountain stood out in sharp greys and purples. 'What can you see up there, Cristoforo?' he asked, staring up into the sky with him.
    'It's not what I *can* see,' the boy said. 'It's what I *can't* see.'
    'Well, then, what *can't* you see?'
    'Birds, Signor Tom. No birds.'
    Patch stared up into the clear sky again, and then it occurred to him with a shock that he had also missed the sleek forms of the swallows, their smooth aerobatics round the houses, and their chattering on the red tiles of the roofs opposite Mamma Meucci's in the early morning before the traffic drowned their cries.
    'That's right,' he said wonderingly, 'there are no swallows. They're late this year.'
    'They're not late, Signor Tom,' Cristoforo said firmly. 'They won't be coming now. They should have arrived long since from Africa and even gone north. They've just not come. Neither have the martins and the orioles and the warblers. The sky's empty.'
    Patch frowned, his mellow mood gone in an instant. He knew immediately that this was another of those odd, inexplicable things that were troubling Hannay, another strange augury of evil.
    'Perhaps it's the heat,' he said. 'It's hot today, Cristoforo.'
    Cristoforo shook his head. 'No, Signor Tom. Not the heat. That would bring them, not send them away.'
    Patch squatted down alongside the boy. 'Cristoforo,' he said seriously, 'have there been any other curious things?'
    'Alfredo Meucci's seen things today, Signor,' Cristoforo said solemnly. 'That's why there's a crowd round his boat. Tomaso's telling everyone now.'
    Patch stared at the noisy group, squinting against the sun. 'What sort of things?'
    'The sea, Signor Tom. Bubbling as though it were boiling. Off Capo Amarea. The Sir Captain's trying to find out what caused it.'
    'Is Captain Hannay there?'

'Yes, Signor. He's at the front of the crowd.'

Patch looked at the group of people for a moment. Somewhere, stirring at the back of his mind, was a distinct uneasiness that he didn't care to admit to, and he straightened himself abruptly.

'Let's go and join them, Cristoforo,' he said.

Hannay looked up as Patch pushed through the crowd. 'You heard what's been happening?' he asked Patch.

Patch nodded and turned to Meucci, who immediately smiled nervously. 'Cristoforo says you've been seeing some pretty strange things, Alfredo,' he said.

Meucci sat silently for a moment, one brown hand resting on the engine, which he wiped slowly with a piece of old rag, almost as though he were leaning on it.

'There was warm water, Signor Tom,' he said cautiously. 'In some places, in fact, it was hot. Hot enough to bubble. And great swells that rose from the bed of the sea and moved without wind.'

Meucci leaned on his rag again. He was remembering a rush of wind about him when there was no wind, and oppressive air in spite of clear sunshine. Then he remembered rumbles coming out to him across the bay, transmitted, it had seemed, by the lifting water – and the freak storm of a few days before which had come smashing down on the startled island out of a clear sky and dazzling visibility.

Meucci looked up at Patch cautiously. 'There have been things,' he said slowly, and went on to explain what he had seen. 'Only last week something frightened the gulls out there by the Capo.'

'What gulls?' Patch found this thing around him – this intangible thing that was beginning to surround them all – was beginning to be creepy.

'They were feeding,' Meucci was saying. 'And suddenly they all flew up into the air.'

'A fish?' Hannay asked. 'Was it a big fish?'

'It was no fish, Signor. There were no fish today. I've been a fisherman all my life and I know when there are fish. I can *smell* fish.'

Patch watched Meucci puffing gratefully at the cigarette he had offered him. The things that were worrying Hannay were beginning to take root in his own mind.

The crowd was silent now, gaping.

'Have these things happened before, Alfredo?' Patch asked.

'Occasionally, Signor Tom. Once now and then. But now they happen all together.'

85 'Do you remember 1892?'

The question seemed to drop like a bomb into the silence. They all knew what the date meant. They all knew of the eruption of the volcano in 1892 and what it had meant.

1. Who first showed signs of worry?

2. Did the continent of Africa lie to the north, south, east or west of these people? Give a reason for your answer.

3. Quote the words between line 9 and line 25 which best indicate that each of these three statements is true:
   a The swallows could not always be heard *all* the time.
   b Patch showed that he was disturbed.
   c The absence of the swallows was not the first strange thing.

4. Give three instances from the first 30 lines which show that Cristoforo had more acute perception than Patch.

5. In line 45 we see that Patch wanted to join the others. Did he have any particular reason?

6. Why do you think that Alfredo smiled nervously and spoke cautiously (lines 48 and 54)?

7. Give two facts about the sea, as observed by Alfredo Meucci, that made 'boiling' an apparently suitable word to use in describing it.

8. Explain the different uses of the apostrophe in 'Meucci's' in line 13 and line 31.

9. Using not more than two words for each, say what the 'things' were that Meucci had seen. Then, again with only two words, say what the conditions were that seemed to make them impossible.

10. To what climax does the author hint that the strange happenings were pointing?

11. What was the final piece of evidence that made Patch suspect what was to happen?

12 On one line, in the last 8 lines of the passage, there is a word and a phrase that mean the same thing. Can you find them?

13 From the whole passage, can you find six phrases to show how Patch's mood progressively changed?

14 In your own words, explain the meaning of:

   a their smooth aerobatics (line 11).
   b to drop like a bomb into the silence (line 86).

15 Give a single word or short phrase that could be substituted for each of the following:

a occurred (line 9)
b inexplicable (line 23)
c augury (line 24)
d uneasiness (line 43)
e oppressive (line 59)
f freak (line 62)
g creepy (line 71)
h gaping (line 81)

22 Fill each blank space with a suitable preposition or adverb particle.

EXAMPLE   All the hotels are completely full up. Could you possibly put me .... the night .... your sofa?

ANSWER   All the hotels are completely full up. Could you possibly put me *up for* the night *on* your sofa?

1 About a quarter .... 1 seven there was great excitement .... 2 the villagers .... 3 Hayslope. Men, women and children had been drawn .... 4 .... 5 their houses .... 6 something more than the pleasure .... 7 being .... 8 the evening sunshine. They stood .... 9 .... 10 little groups, all .... 11 them curious to see the young female teacher.
(From *Adam Bede*, by George Eliot)

2 We started .... 1 .... 2 the early morning. The car had stood .... 3 the house all night, and we were .... 4 a few minutes .... 5 five o'clock, ... 6 the intention .... 7 going as far possible before the roads filled .... 8 .... 9 the early morning traffic. It was 200 miles .... 10 the cottage that Phyllis had bought and settled .... 11 .... 12 .... 13 the South.
(From *The Kraken Wakes*, by John Wyndham)

3 Barrett staggered .... 1 the front door and dropped the two enormous suitcases .... 2 .... 3 the hall floor. Painfully, he straightened .... 4 and stretched his body. He stood still .... 5 a few moments, feeling the ache .... 6 his shoulders die .... 7. He went unsteadily .... 8 the living-room, walked .... 9 .... 10 the sofa and flopped .... 11 .... 12 it. His heart was still beating .... 13 a blacksmith's hammer .... 14 a piece of iron.
(From *The Tell-Tale*, by Robert Long)

4 'I'm surprised you're going .... 1 that hotel,' said Hadley. 'I don't know how you can put .... 2 .... 3 it. I was there again last week, but never again! The service was never .... 4 .... 5 much, but it's really disgraceful now. .... 6 my first night I arrived too late .... 7 dinner, so I went .... 8 .... 9 my room about ten o'clock and rang the room-service .... 10 some sandwiches and a bottle .... 11 beer. I waited .... 12 midnight and then I gave it .... 13. I got .... 14 bed hungry and went .... 15 sleep. .... 16 about half-past twelve there was a knock .... 17 the door and a waiter presented me .... 18 the sandwiches and the beer. No apology .... 19 all. You can understand I didn't feel .... 20 giving the waiter any tip, but he stood .... 21 the doorway with his hand half held .... 22 .... 23 front .... 24 him. Weakly, I gave .... 25 simply to get rid .... 26 him!

(From *One Efficient Person,* by John Millington Ward)

5 It was just a week exactly since Mr Martin had decided to deal .... 1 Mrs Ulgine Barrows. He called it 'rubbing .... 2' Mrs Barrows. The words pleased him because they suggested nothing more than the correction .... 3 a mistake. Mr Martin had spent each night .... 4 the past week working .... 5 his plan and examining it. As he walked home now he went .... 6 it again.

(From *The Catbird Seat,* by James Thurber)

6 Floating .... 1 .... 2 the air, fairly .... 3 the ground, there are millions .... 4 particles .... 5 dust. The dust may be made .... 6 .... 7 smoke .... 8 fires, tiny seeds .... 9 plants, even bits .... 10 soil. You can see these particles .... 11 dust lit .... 12 .... 13 a stream .... 14 sunlight which comes .... 15 .... 16 a window or a crack .... 17 the wall. Scientists have made experiments to find .... 18 how much dust there is .... 19 the air .... 20 various places. .... 21 a dirty town one cubic metre .... 22 air may contain thousands .... 23 millions .... 24 particles.

(From *The Air Around Us,* by W. E. Flood)

43

7 I was .... 1 a small port .... 2 Burma, and .... 3 there I took the steamship .... 4 Mandalay. Two days .... 5 our arrival, when the boat was tied .... 6 .... 7 the night .... 8 a riverside village, I made .... 9 my mind to go ashore. The Captain had told me I could drop .... 10 .... 11 a countryman of mine, a missionary .... 12 sorts, who would be delighted to see me and who had a good supply .... 13 gin, something the bar .... 14 board was sadly short .... 15.

(From *Mabel,* by W. Somerset Maugham)

8 We began to make our way .... 1 a small forest. I was tired .... 2 .... 3 this time. I was also wet .... 4 perspiration, and I took .... 5 my warm coat. Demyan glided .... 6 .... 7 a boat, his snow-shoes never catching .... 8 anything nor slipping .... 9. He even took my coat .... 10 me and slung it .... 11 his own shoulder, and still kept urging me .... 12.

(From *The Bear Hunt,* by Leo Tolstoy)

9 As Gabriel walked .... 1, and the voice drew nearer, he found .... 2 that it came .... 3 a small boy who, to keep himself company .... 4 the dark, was shouting .... 5 his song .... 6 the highest pitch .... 7 his lungs. So Gabriel waited until the boy came .... 8 .... 9 him, and then pushed him .... 10 a corner and knocked him .... 11 the head .... 12 his lantern to teach him to be quieter. The boy ran .... 13 .... 14 the road, ... 15 his hands .... 16 his head, singing a different sort .... 17 tune.

(From *The Goblin and the Gravedigger,* by Charles Dickens)

10 .... 1 despair, cold sharp despair, buried deep .... 2 her heart .... 3 a wicked knife, Miss Meadows, ... 4 cap and gown and carrying a little baton, trod .... 5 the cold corridors that led .... 6 .... 7 the music hall. Girls .... 8 all ages, rosy .... 9 the air, and bubbling .... 10 .... 11 that gleeful excitement that comes .... 12 running .... 13 school .... 14 a fine autumn morning, hurried, skipped, fluttered .... 15.

(From *The Singing Lesson,* by Katherine Mansfield)

23 Change the direct speech in these sentences into reported speech.

EXAMPLE   'Let's all go to the cinema tomorrow,' said my mother.
ANSWER   My mother suggested that we should all go to the cinema the next day.

1 'I'm sorry about it,' the policeman said to us, 'but I shall have to give you a ticket. You must surely have known that parking is absolutely forbidden anywhere in this street.'

2 'I feel rather faint,' said Aunt Bertha. 'I don't think I can go on. But you go on without me, all of you. I'll just sit here till you come back. I'll be perfectly all right.'

3 'Why don't you go and push a baby-carriage?' the taxi-driver said to the other driver angrily. 'You're not fit to drive a car.'

4 I heard the nurse say to him, 'Do lie still. You'll pull your stitches open if you keep moving about like that.'

5 Jason said to his wife, 'Well, if you really do want to wear that awful skirt, I suppose I can't stop you. But it makes you look like a sack of potatoes.'

6 The judge said to the man in the dock, 'Did you ask for, or receive, permission to use a company car that night?'

7 Harry said to his wife, 'I'm going to see my mother this evening if I can get away from the office a little earlier. Have you any messages for her?'

8 'If you really think I said that about you,' said Charles, 'I'm not surprised that you're angry with me. But I assure you I did not.'

9 Rosemary said to Stephen, 'What very old-fashioned ideas you have! We're not living in the eighteenth century. You talk as though women should be seen and not heard. I'm glad you're not *my* husband, I must say.'

10 'Let me help you with that suitcase,' Timothy said to the pretty girl at the station. 'It looks a lot too heavy for you.'

11 'Hold these wires carefully,' said the electrician to his assistant. 'We don't want to get a shock with *this* voltage!'

12 'We'd better bring some warmer clothes with us next time we come here,' said my father. 'It gets a lot colder in winter than I realised.'

13 'There's no sense,' said my wife to me, with amusement in her eyes, 'in your getting all worn out chasing a bat with a fly-swatter. They are much quicker than you are.'

14 'You will really have to have your hair cut soon,' Polly said to Walter. 'You're beginning to look uncouth.'

15 Marilyn said, 'I'm terribly sorry I'm so late. I wish I could learn to look at the clock. Do please forgive me.'

16 'What a beauty!' said Victor, gazing at the Rolls-Royce outside the hotel.

17 Phyllis said severely to her husband, 'What have you been cutting with my scissors?'

18 'Go away,' Sylvia said to the gypsy, who had his foot in the door. 'Otherwise I will scream – and the next-door neighbour will come running.'

19 'As it happens,' said Basil, with dignity. 'I came here to do you a favour, not to ask for one.'

20 'Why were you wearing that medal?' said the police inspector. 'You have no right to it. You have never been in any of the services.'

24 The numbered blank spaces in this passage are each followed by three words in parentheses. In some cases, all three of these words could be used to fill the blank spaces; in other cases, only two could be used; in other cases, only one. Make your choice now.

.... 1 (If / Whether / Whenever) we want to see how civilisation .... 2 (develops / grows / produces), to .... 3 (see / watch / look) the process actually operating, we .... 4 (need / must / should) only observe the first few years' .... 5 (process / development / progress) of an individual citizen. Every child starts life as a primitive savage, and then, by contact with others, becomes progressively
.... 6 (little / less / few) of the little barbarian he was born. He learns the 7
(conventions / bureaucracies / formalities)
imposed by .... 8 (community / communist / communal) life, and gradually .... 9 (approaches / comes / arrives) to .... 10 (appreciate / estimate / value) them. It has sometimes been .... 11 (maintained / said / claimed), by cynics and lately by rebellious adolescents, that the disciplines on which civilised life is .... 12 (based / standing / stood) are just a kind of .... 13 (selfishness / meanness / thoughtlessness), ... 14 (merely / purely / simply) a clever way of .... 15 (assuring / ensuring / insuring) that some sections of society get what they want without fuss or challenge. An alternative and perhaps healthier .... 16 (view / panorama / aspect) is that mutual tolerance is the way in which .... 17 (individuals / people / one) can realise the best in themselves and develop to the .... 18 (top / full / head) their particular .... 19 (talents / gifts / presents) and .... 20 (potentialities / probabilities / capabilities).

25 Rephrase each of these sentences in such a way that you can include the word that appears in capital letters. Do not alter this word in any way.

EXAMPLE Has she written to you lately? HEARD
ANSWER   Have you heard from her lately?

1 We must have your answer tonight at the latest. INSIST
2 My father is going to lend me his car tonight. BORROW
3 We've decided to replace those plastic shower curtains with these rubber ones. SUBSTITUTE
4 Somebody has stolen all Miranda's jewellery. ROBBED
5 You don't mean to say you want a fifth icecream, do you? SURELY
6 The bank now owns this block of flats. BELONGS
7 He was speaking so quickly that I couldn't understand him. TOO
8 The fridge is absolutely empty. LEFT
9 He was not listening to what we were saying. PAYING
10 Nothing ever frightens him. AFRAID
11 It's not my habit to get up quite so early as this. USED
12 Can you tell me the way to the Central Post Office? DIRECT
13 Everything went well that morning. NOTHING
14 Why did you do that? FOR
15 Nanette talks about her illnesses all the time. NEVER
16 Only the fact that I found a taxi quickly enabled me to catch the train. IF
17 A portion of strawberries and cream costs a lot in the café. CHARGES
18 How likely am I to pass the examination, do you think? CHANCE
19 Humphrey doesn't like cocktail parties. It's a waste of time, asking him. POINT
20 Please throw all these things away. RID

26 Here are a number of sentences with either positive or negative results. Making sure that the meanings remain the same, rephrase those with a positive result by using the adverb *enough*, and those with a negative result by using the adverb *too*.

EXAMPLE 1 Martin is so rich that he *can* buy whatever he wants.
ANSWER   Martin is rich *enough* to buy whatever he wants.
EXAMPLE 2 Edna is so impatient that she can *never* wait in queues.
ANSWER   Edna is *too* impatient ever to wait in queues.

1 Howard was so suspicious of his wife that he opened the letter that was addressed to her.
2 The balcony was so badly built that it was not safe for people to stand on.
3 This hotel is so expensive that we can't stay at it for very long.
4 Erica is so careful that she could not have done anything as bad as that.
5 Your feet are so small, Madam, that you can wear the smallest of our sizes.
6 Barry was so strong that he lifted the trunk on to the top of the car alone.
7 Hazel's new American car is so wide that it won't go into her garage easily.
8 Ray is free this evening. He will help you.
9 The sky was so cloudy that we couldn't see the UFO at all.
10 It was so late that nothing could be done.
11 This little hotel is so quiet and peaceful that we can have a really relaxing holiday.
12 Jessica is so cruel that she might have been a pupil of Messalina.
13 Let's go to another beach. There are so many jelly-fish here that we shan't be able to bathe in peace.
14 Please write this again, Felix. It is written so badly that I cannot make sense of it.

15 Richard is so tall that he can change light bulbs in some rooms without having to stand on a chair.

16 It was so late when we arrived at the hotel that no food could be cooked for us.

17 Vera knows her husband's habits and movements so well that she can say where he is and what he is doing at any moment.

18 This restaurant has become so expensive that few people use it.

19 The carpet was so dirty that we could not clean it.

20 Mother says she's getting rather elderly. She can't wear a bikini any longer.

27 On the left below is a list of people and on the right a list of things, each arranged alphabetically. Say which thing could logically be associated with a person. Choose only one thing for each person.

1	baker	a	cardiograph
2	carpenter	b	drill
3	conductor	c	goggles
4	dentist	d	handcuffs
5	electrician	e	lathe
6	farmer	f	notepad
7	gardener	g	oven
8	glazier	h	pipe
9	heart specialist	i	plough
10	jockey	j	pulpit
11	motor-cyclist	k	putty
12	nurse	l	rostrum
13	plumber	m	rubber gloves
14	policeman	n	saw
15	priest	o	spade
16	railway porter	p	thermometer
17	secretary	q	thread
18	surgeon	r	trolley
19	tailor	s	whip
20	toolmaker	t	wire

28 Read this passage, and then look at the exercise that follows it.

The sun was shining quite brightly as Mrs Grant left her house, and she saw no need to take an umbrella with her. She got on the bus to take her into the town and before long it came on to rain. It had not stopped when the bus arrived at the market-place half an hour later. Mrs Grant stood up and absent-mindedly picked up the umbrella that was hanging on the seat in front of her.

A cold voice said loudly: 'That is mine, Madam!'

Suddenly remembering that she had come out without her umbrella, Mrs Grant blushed with embarrassment and apologised, trying at the same time to ignore the unpleasant look the owner of the umbrella was giving her.

When she got off the bus, Mrs Grant made straight for a shop where she could buy an umbrella. She found a very pretty one and, because it was so pretty, decided to buy another as a present for her daughter. She did the rest of her shopping and had lunch in a café.

In the afternoon she got on the homeward bus with the two umbrellas under her arm, and sat down. Then she saw that, by a curious coincidence, she was sitting next to the woman who had made her feel so uncomfortable that morning.

This woman now looked at her, then at the umbrellas, and said, 'You've had quite a good day, I see.'

Here are some sentences from the passage with a number of words or phrases printed in *italics*. Rephrase each of these sentences in such a way that you keep the original meaning but *do not use any word or phrase that is printed in italics*. You may freely take away other words that are not in italics, or you may add new words, but you must make sure that the sentence remains grammatically correct.

In some cases a simple synonym may be all that is needed:

EXAMPLE   The bus *arrived* at the market-place.
ANSWER   The bus *reached* the market-place.

In other cases a change of construction and the use of different words may be needed:

EXAMPLE   'That is *mine*, Madam!'
ANSWER   'That *belongs to me*, Madam!'

1. The sun was shining quite brightly *as* Mrs Grant left her *house*.
2. She *saw no need* to take an umbrella with her.
3. *Before long* it *came on to* rain.
4. It *had not stopped* when the bus arrived at the market-place.
5. Mrs Grant absentmindedly *picked up* the umbrella that was hanging on the seat *in front* of her.
6. Mrs Grant *blushed* with embarrassment and *apologised*.
7. She tried to *ignore* the unpleasant look the owner of the umbrella was giving her.
8. Mrs Grant *made straight for* a shop where she *could buy* an umbrella.
9. She found a very pretty one and, because it was *so* pretty, decided to buy *another* as a present for her daughter.
10. She did the *rest* of her shopping and *had* lunch in a café.

29 Can you say what these capital letters stand for?

EXAMPLE B.B.C.
ANSWER   British Broadcasting Corporation

1 A.D.	6 M.P.	11 S.O.S.
2 B.C.	7 N.A.T.O.	12 U.K.
3 C.I.A.	8 P.S.	13 U.N.E.S.C.O.
4 C.I.D.	9 P.T.O.	14 U.N.O.
5 M.A.	10 R.S.V.P.	15 Y.M.C.A.

30 Finish each of the incomplete sentences below in such a way that it has the same meaning as the sentence which is printed above it.

EXAMPLE It would be wise for us to take raincoats.
         We'd ....
ANSWER   We'd better take raincoats.

1 It is said that he escaped to a neutral country.
   He ....

2 Oil was slowly covering the sand of the beach.
   The sand of the beach ....

3 In spite of all our efforts, we failed.
   Although ....

4 We'd prefer you not to wear those slippers in the office, Miss Blake.
   We'd rather ....

5 The storm blew the roof off the house.
   The house ....

6 You really should be able to dress yourself by now, Elsie.
   It's time you ....

7 This is the quickest way to get into the centre of the city.
   There's ....

8 Only one person knew what had caused the fire.
   The cause ....

9 I don't think this punch-bowl has enough brandy in it.
   There is too ....

10 Provided your handwriting is legible, the examiners will accept your paper.
 So long as the examiners ....

11 I'll take a mackintosh because it may rain this evening.
 In case ....

12 There are a lot of people dependent on him.
 He ....

13 What I admire most about him is his absolute frankness.
 His absolute frankness, more ....

14 How did you get the idea that they're rich?
 What made ....?

15 We could have done more for them really.
 We didn't ....

16 I won't keep you long. I know you're in a hurry.
 I won't take up ....

17 As one grows older one becomes more intolerant.
 The older ....

18 The fourth time he asked her to marry him, she accepted.
 Only on his fourth ....

19 Immediately after his arrival home a water-heater exploded.
 Hardly ....

20 Patricia loves Mozart, and above all his operas.
 Patricia loves Mozart, but what ....

31 The word in capital letters at the end of each of these sentences can be changed in such a way that it forms a word that fits suitably in the blank space. Fill each blank in this way.

EXAMPLE The bloodstain on her dress was very .... NOTICE
ANSWER   The bloodstain on her dress was very *noticeable*.

1 I'm surprised at what you've done. I hope my confidence in you has not been .... PLACE

2 Fresh vegetables certainly have a better taste than .... ones. FREEZE

3 All .... should go to Room 24. APPLY

4 That painting is not just extremely valuable, it is .... PRICE

5 To avoid .... on the journey we'd better pack these glasses in either cotton wool or soft paper. BREAK

6 If you don't put the proper stamps on the envelope, the .... will have to pay double when he receives the letter. RECEIVE

7 The cat looked at the new type of food on its plate .... SUSPECT

8 No, Shirley, that sort of dress is quite .... for a wedding. SUIT

9 .... his working life he has been dreaming of being able to retire on a farm. THROUGH

10 Tom gave the .... a pound. BEG

11 Poor Quentin put his head too far out of the railway carriage window and was .... by a passing train. HEAD

12 Any bright light at night is an .... to mosquitoes. ATTRACT

13 This is no longer a quiet residential .... NEIGHBOUR

14 How awful! What an .... thing for anyone to do! OUTRAGE

15 The runner was so fast and so good that he won the race quite .... EFFORT

16 I didn't get the job because I didn't have the right .... QUALIFY

17 The Government is going to hold a .... to find out what the people really think about the proposal. REFER

18 Theodore has a very sweet .... smile. CHILD

19 Some friends arrived .... last night, so we all went out to dinner. EXPECT

20 Make sure that you .... the electricity before you start mending this light switch. CONNECT

55

32 Make all the changes and additions necessary to produce, from the following groups of words and phrases, a complete letter from Natalie to her friend Belinda. (See Exercise 7 for an example, if necessary.)

Dear Belinda,

Thank you / letter / arrive / yesterday
1 ....

Postmark / show / it / post / more / three weeks
2 ....

How bad / postal services / become / recently / really awful!
3 ....

Anyway / not much news / tell you / everything quiet / here
4 ....

Except / one thing / perhaps / interest / you
5 ....

Daughter Jane / tell us / yesterday / she and Ronald / decide / have wedding / St. George's / month's time
6 ....
....

They say / want / very quiet wedding / so / invite / only few / people
7 ....

Not decide yet / where live / but we / hope / it / near us
8 ....

If Jane / need / come London / buy / wedding dress / can you / put up / for night?
9 ....
....

However / feel sure / she / write / you herself / ask you / if need / arise
10 ....

Yours ever,

Natalie

33 Fill each of the numbered blank spaces in this passage with ONE suitable word.

Peter Merrill stood at a window of Rome Airport and watched the graceful descent of the aircraft that was .... 1 his wife. When he saw that all its .... 2 were safely on the .... 3, he turned .... 4 into the reception room and sat down to .... 5.

Susan and he .... 6 married three weeks before. Two days after their wedding, she had a telegram from home saying that her mother was ill and she had .... 7 to fly to London .... 8. He had been .... 9 to go with her, for he was a teacher at the Parker Institute and it was the middle of the academic year. So he had stayed .... 10, spending most of his .... 11 time at his club because the emptiness of the bed-sitting-room home at the Anconi Hotel depressed him.

After only a quarter of an hour or .... 12, having .... 13 very quickly with the customs and immigration formalities, Susan came to him and they .... 14 their way to the car park.

'Anything exciting happened while I've been .... 15?' asked Susan, as they set off for the centre of Rome.

'My contract's been .... 16 for another year,' said Peter.

'Oh good. I wanted to stay on for a bit longer. .... 17 else?' Peter glanced at her. 'I've taken a furnished flat for us.'

'Have you indeed?' she said after a short pause.

'I hope you .... 18 of the idea,' he said quickly. 'If we were going to be here only for the rest of this term, we could've stayed on at the hotel. But another full year there ... I don't think we could have .... 19 it, in spite of the wonderful restaurant.'

'Well, well,' she said. 'Life is full of surprises! It's a lovely idea, darling. There's one problem, ... 20.'

'What's that?'

'I'll have to learn how to cook.'

57

34 Change each of the following sentences in such a way as to avoid using the word or phrase that is printed in *italics*, either by omitting it or by replacing it with one suitable word.

EXAMPLE 1   Which would you prefer? English beer or German *beer*?
ANSWER   Which would you prefer? English beer or German?

EXAMPLE 2   Is that a leather handbag or a plastic *handbag*?
ANSWER   Is that a leather handbag or a plastic *one*?

1   What time is the news on the TV? I want to see *the news*.

2   I'd love to have a car like that, but I'll never be able to afford *a car like that*.

3   Where are my scissors? Have you seen *my scissors*?

4   The only person Helen is interested in is *Helen*.

5   The women at that bank seem to be more helpful than the men *at that bank*.

6   Yes, I like shrimps very much but I prefer the North Sea *shrimps* to the Mediterranean *shrimps*.

7   The price of petrol is now more expensive than *the price of petrol* should be, considering the drop in the price of crude oil.

8   People who do things are more interesting than *people* who just talk about *doing things*.

9   Last month the value of gold rose more sharply than *the value* of platinum.

10 The rain seems to be stopping. At least, I hope *the rain seems to be stopping*.

11 Our football team is leaving at 2 o'clock. Shall we go to the airport to see *our football team* off?

12 I wonder if there is going to be another earthquake. I very much hope *there is* not *going to be another earthquake*.

13 There are two very significant facts about this case that I must tell you about. The *first very significant fact* concerns your wife and the *second very significant fact* concerns your brother-in-law.

14 Here is my umbrella and there is Tom's *umbrella*.

15 I'm afraid I have got very low marks in Mathematics again. *Mathematics* can't be called my best subject!

35 Here is a sentence without capital letters and without punctuation:

james said do you agree with those people and there are very many of them arent there who say that mozarts best opera is the magic flute

Correctly punctuated and presented, it becomes:

James said, "Do you agree with those people – and there are very many of them, aren't there? – who say that Mozart's best opera is 'The Magic Flute'?"

Here, now, is a passage for you to punctuate and present correctly, with capital letters where necessary, and suitable paragraphs.

the red warning light appeared on the wall of the aeroplane beside the pilots head as i saw it my heart gave another jump here we are sir said the dispatcher cheerfully he got up from his seat and opened the sliding door there was a terrifying noise the air outside seemed to be screaming furiously at us i felt very frightened again i tried to calm myself by remembering what the instructor had said during the weeks of training no matter how often you jump youll never lose the fear of it as you get yourself ready but dont feel ashamed of it its very natural everybody feels afraid i got up and approached the open doorway i put my hands on its sides and gripped i did not look down at the earth i stared straight out into space chewed on my gum felt sick and waited seeing the red light from the corner of my eyes the red light went out the green one came on the dispatcher behind me said ready sir i nodded my head okay then he said one two three go

36

Here are twenty sentences each with a blank space. Below each one are four words. Choose which one of these most suitably fills the blank space.

1. You should .... a lawyer before you sign that document.
   counsel   check   consult   communicate

2. We couldn't have our picnic because it began to .... with rain.
   flow   drench   run   pour

3. My brother is a parachute ....
   trainer   teacher   educator   instructor

4. We can no longer afford the cost of .... two cars, so we're selling one.
   operating   managing   running   controlling

5. I don't .... what people think about the way I dress.
   matter   care   attend   concern

6. You can't compare those two hotels. They're not in the same ....
   form   class   band   set

7. I enjoy working as his secretary, but he is such a perfectionist that it's ....
   exhausting   exhaustive   fatigued   sleepy

8. It is becoming more and more .... that the Government has lost the confidence of the nation.
   understood   apparent   anticipated   expected

9. In the summer we often sleep in the .... air on our terrace.
   clear   clean   open   full

10. The taxi-drivers are complaining that their fares are too ....
    small   little   low   few

11. He swatted a fly on the window and .... the glass.
    slashed   smashed   cut   crashed

12. A walnut tree .... us from the sun on hot days.
    fences   warns   shelters   prevents

13 Do be careful not to .... your coffee on this white rug, Bill.
    drip spill filter leak

14 Nobody .... that aeroplane crash.
    survived recovered lived released

15 The Queen has said that she will .... the ceremony.
    engage come attend impart

16 It is strange that Lucy is as .... as her mother is beautiful.
    dull plain humble raw

17 His request .... me completely by surprise.
    left shook made took

18 Their last cook was better than their .... one.
    current former latter instant

19 I wanted to go home but my girlfriend .... on going to a nightclub.
    persisted insisted demanded intended

20 She likes to sit on the balcony and .... what goes on below.
    look gaze glare watch

37 Rearrange the order of words in these sentences in such a way that each of them becomes a correctly expressed question.

EXAMPLE the say you time is what did?
ANSWER   What did you say the time is?

1 lottery buy if what you would a you won

2 light please out won't turn the you the hall in

3 this holiday our summer for we go shall where

4 between human difference is and the humane what

5 milk should buy how tins of think you many do we

6 would earth telephone why late so say to be on you didn't you

7 one that I shall dress or buy this

61

8   have people many how the accepted invitation

9   today library time does the what close

10 obstinate that anyone you could believe can so stupid and be

11 shoes your towel a dare again with you did clean to

12 landowner year close why road once that the does every

13 wear going for to are you costume of ball what fancy-dress the sort

14 much has sink seen collected how in the you have washing-up kitchen

15 bed after stay doctor in operation the long to have I think you shall how do

38 Say the words in these twenty pairs aloud, paying particular attention to where the strong stress lies.

1   advertiser – advertisement
2   ambiguous – ambiguity
3   architecture – architectural
4   benefit – beneficial
5   catholic – catholicism
6   celebrate – celebrity
7   ceremony – ceremonial
8   contribution – contributory
9   courage – courageous
10 domestic – domesticity
11 horizon – horizontal
12 individual – individuality
13 information – informative
14 managerial – management
15 medicine – medicinal
16 necessary – necessity
17 obligation – obligatory
18 professional – professorial
19 radiator – radiation
20 solemn – solemnity

39 Change the infinitives that are in brackets in these sentences into either the (active or passive) Past Simple or Past Perfect, according to what is required in English usage.

1   By the time Bill left school, he (learn) good French and German. When he was at university he (learn) Italian and Spanish.

2   Cecil Fisher, the jeweller, (charge) yesterday with being in possession of stolen property. The police (allege) that most

of Lady Clarence's jewellery – stolen by burglars a month ago – (find) in his shop.

3 The Blakeways (be) very late. The Beethoven Ninth Symphony (play) by the time they (reach) the concert hall. They (be) very disappointed to find that they (miss) it.

4 When our friends (arrive) we (go) into the garden. We (find) we couldn't use the canvas chairs, though. It (rain) heavily the night before and I (forget) to put them under cover.

5 Neville had to wait in the street until his wife (come) home. It (be) his own fault. He (forget) again to take his keys with him.

6 When I (return) to where I (park) my car, it (not be) there. At first, I (think) it (steal), but soon I (learn) that the police (tow) it away.

7 Because Jasper (make) an appointment with his dentist he (hope) he would not have to wait very long, although there (be) a lot of people in the waiting-room when he (arrive).

8 Zoe (not want) to come to my wedding. It (be) obvious from the moment she (arrive) at the church. I (hear) later that her brother (persuade) her to come. She (stand) in a corner, unsmiling and unfriendly. I (think) she (be) a thoroughly unpleasant person. I (not speak) to her.

9 To my very great surprise, my father (allow) me to drive his Rolls-Royce yesterday. For a long time I (hope) he might one day do so, but I never (believe) it would happen. You can imagine my feelings, then, when he (give) me the key and (tell) me to take over. It (be) a wonderful experience.

10 About six o'clock in the evening we (find) ourselves at the foot of the Rosetta Pass. Earlier in the day we (see) no reason why we should not reach San Martino before dark, but some unlucky happenings (delay) us. The most difficult part of the journey (be) still in front of us, and the sinking sun (warn) us it would be unwise to go on. Rather against our will we (decide) to spend the night at the Mountaineers' Hut on the pass itself.

40 Examine these three sentences:

a Loretta explained the problem surprisingly clearly.
b Loretta explained the problem with surprising clarity.
c Loretta's explanation of the problem was surprisingly clear.

All express the same meaning with nearly the same words, but with some difference of form. Below are ten sentences, each phrased on the model of the first sentence above (a). Give the other two phrasings for all of them.

1 Lorna laughed extremely nervously.
2 The shop assistant answered my wife very rudely.
3 The policeman did not give his evidence at the trial completely honestly.
4 The boss replied to me rather ironically.
5 Uncle Jerry lent the money slightly unwillingly.
6 The medicine reacted most unpleasantly.
7 The mechanic repaired my car extremely inefficiently.
8 I'm afraid you behaved astonishingly stupidly.
9 Aunt Fanny cut the birthday cake into eight equal pieces very carefully.
10 Francis acted quite absent-mindedly again.

41 In each of these sentences there is one mistake. Can you find it, and can you give the correct version?

1 Painted bright red, Jack always finds his bicycle quickly amongst all the others outside the factory.

2 The bus was plenty of people who had spent many a happy hour in the stores doing their Christmas shopping.

3 Do sit down for a little bit, Julian. It is since breakfast that you are doing this heavy digging – and that is over four hours now.

4 I wasn't invited to their party, for some reason or other. I should very much have liked to have gone. I hear it was a great success.

5 Those oysters that ate my brother last night in that so-charming little sea-front restaurant must have been polluted. He is very off-colour this morning.

6 I regret having to tell you that I'll have to be away from the office for a while next week. My dentist has found I've got pyorrhoea in my gums and I've finally got to take out all my teeth. I'll be back as soon as I can.

7 The whole family went over the Channel to Calais for the day last weekend. The crossing was so rough, though, that nobody but my father and I really enjoyed the outing. All the others were seasick, both going and coming.

8 You're not looking your best, Edwin. Let me feel your forehead. Yes, you certainly have a temperature. I'd think you'd better not to go to school today.

9 In the last thirty years the man has invented some remarkably effective means of destroying not only himself but also everything else on the planet.

10 Again the Johnsons arrived at the opera late, and again they were not allowed to go in until the end of the first act. It served them right, of course. If only they left their house ten minutes earlier they would have arrived in good time.

42 The two sentences *Chloe carelessly disregarded the instructions on the medicine bottle* and *This almost killed her* can be combined into one sentence by replacing the verb of the first sentence with a suitable noun and by omitting the word *This* from the second sentence; i.e. *Chloe's careless disregard of the instructions on the medicine bottle almost killed her.*

Combine these pairs of sentences in the same way, but try to avoid using the noun *-ing* form. Make whatever other changes are needed.

1 The policeman was unwilling to listen to the old lady's explanation. This made her very angry.
2 The girl persuasively denied that she had stolen anything. This made her boss believe her.
3 I obeyed your instructions very carefully. This brought about a perfect result.
4 My parents obviously did not like my new boyfriend. This prevented me from inviting him home very often.
5 Nina impulsively bought a diamond necklace yesterday. This may cause her to abandon her holiday plans.
6 The tree grew rapidly. This was partly the result of our constant care of it.
7 Dennis recently lost a leg in an accident. This is the reason why he has to move around in a wheelchair.
8 My brother feared heights. This was well known to me.
9 Jackson disobeyed an order from an officer. This caused his arrest.
10 She believed in me. This encouraged me in spite of every difficulty.
11 We have discovered uranium on our land. This may make us rich.
12 The audience behaved calmly when the bomb went off. This prevented a panic and a catastrophe.
13 That nurse was terribly careless. This cannot be excused.

14 The Army does not approve of long hair. This surprises very few people.

15 The Prime Minister sharply criticised the rebellious members of her party. This didn't make any difference.

43 Fill each of the blank spaces in these sentences with ONE of the following particles.

AFTER   BY   INTO   OFF   OVER   ROUND   THROUGH   WITH

1 The prisoner fainted under the torture but came .... when they threw a bucket of ice-cold water over him.

2 Would you look .... these rather valuable things for us while we're away?

3 Christina came .... a huge fortune when her father died.

4 I saw Linda in the town this morning and she asked .... you.

5 You can keep the book if you want. I've finished .... it.

6 The Densons have had to call .... their party because Elaine is ill.

7 Do you think I have any chance of getting .... my driving test?

8 If we don't pay the bill tomorrow, they'll cut .... our electricity.

9 What are you going to do .... all this wood you have bought?

10 The judge was very kind. Emma got .... with a £10 fine.

11 Fiona won a lot of money in a sweepstake but ran .... it in six months.

12 How did you ever get .... that policeman to let you park here?

13 I'm handing the post .... to my successor at the end of the month.

14 Let me quickly look ………… this catalogue to see if there's anything nice.

15 Patsy seems to have got ………… her shyness at last.

16 I don't speak the language at all well. I just manage to get ………… .

17 Who do you think we ran ………… at the theatre last night?

18 As the years go …………, one learns to be less demanding of life.

19 You'd better have nothing to do ………… him. He is a complete rogue.

20 I can't imagine what I said to upset her, but she suddenly burst ………… tears.

44 Read through this passage, and then do the exercise that follows it.

　　The chemist* woke up, switched on the light beside his head, and looked at the clock. A quarter to four.
　　The knocking on the door of the shop downstairs was repeated.
5　　'Blast!' said the chemist. He got out of bed, put on his dressing-gown and slippers, and went heavily down to the shop. He unbolted and opened the door. In the street was a man who was swaying a little from side to side.
　　'What can I do for you?' said the chemist, forcing some
10　politeness into his voice. 'Are you ill?'
　　'Good evening,' said the man, smiling. 'Or, rather, good morning.' A strong smell of alcohol came from his mouth. 'No, I'm not ill. I simply need a bottle of ink.'
　　'A bottle of what?'
15　'Ink.'
　　The chemist stared at him. 'Good God!' he said disbelievingly. He felt his anger rising. 'Are you too drunk to see that this is a chemist's?'
　　The man looked at him blankly. 'A chemist's?'
20　'Yes,' shouted the chemist. 'And chemists do not sell ink.'

*chemist: pharmacist

'Oh dear,' said the man. 'Never?'

'Of course not!' shouted the chemist. 'In twenty years of running this shop, I have never had any ink. Go away and get lost!'

'Oh dear,' said the man compassionately. 'Twenty years without any ink. That's awful.'

A window on the other side of the street opened. A voice yelled:

'Shut up! It's the middle of the night!'

The man put his finger to his lips. 'Shsss!' he said.

The chemist shut the door with a slam like an explosion and stamped back upstairs to his bedroom.

'Who was it, dear?' asked his wife sleepily. 'Why were you shouting so much? You must have woken the whole street up.'

'A drunk wanting a bottle of ink.'

His wife laughed lightly into her pillow.

The chemist glared at her. 'What's funny?'

'I thought you said a bottle of ink, dear.'

'I did say a bottle of ink,' shouted the chemist. 'And it isn't funny.' He flung off his dressing-gown, kicked his slippers the length of the room, and climbed back into bed, cursing.

An hour later, his wife shook him awake. 'Oswald, there's someone knocking again.'

The chemist raised his head and listened. 'No,' he said. 'Absolutely not. I'm not going down again. Let him find an all-night chemist's, whoever he is.'

'Oswald,' said his wife. 'It might be something serious. I do think you ought to go down and see, dear.'

The chemist spoke a number of bad words, and got heavily out of bed. He began to search for his slippers. When at last he found them, one under the wardrobe, the other behind the dressing-table, he made his way down to the shop.

Outside in the street was the man who had come before. 'Hello,' he said. 'Hello, hello!'

The chemist began to shake with fury.

'I came back as quickly as I could,' said the man. 'I hope you hadn't gone back to sleep.' He took from a pocket a small parcel. 'I found the ink. And since you haven't had any for twenty years I bought a bottle for you, too.'

Here are some sentences from the passage with a number of words or phrases in *italics*. Rephrase each of the sentences in such a way that you keep the original meaning, but do not use any word or phrase that is printed in italics. You may freely take away other words that are not in italics, or you may add new words, but you must make sure that the sentence remains grammatically correct.

In some cases a simple synonym may be all that is needed:
EXAMPLE   The man looked at him *blankly*.
ANSWER   The man looked at him *expressionlessly (vacantly, etc.)*

In other cases, a change of the construction or of other words may be needed:
EXAMPLE   A strong smell of alcohol *came from his mouth*.
ANSWER   His breath smelled strongly of alcohol.

1 The knocking on the door of the shop downstairs *was repeated*.

2 'What can I *do for* you?' said the chemist. . . .

3 . . . forcing some politeness *into his voice*.

4 'Good evening,' said the man, smiling. 'Or *rather* good morning.'

5 'I *simply need* a bottle of ink.'

6 'Are you *too* drunk to see that this is a chemist's?'

7 'In twenty years of *running this shop* I have never had any ink.'

8 'Oh dear,' said the man compassionately. 'Twenty years without *any* ink.'

9 The chemist shut the door with a slam *like* an explosion.

10 '*Why* were you shouting so much?'

11 'You must have woken *the whole street* up.'

12 His wife laughed *lightly* into her pillow.

13 The chemist glared at her. 'What's *funny*?'

14 He kicked his slippers the *length* of the room.

He climbed *back* into bed, cursing.

'Let him find an all-night chemist's, who*ever* he is.'

The chemist *spoke a number of bad words.*

He *made his way* down to the shop again.

'I came back as quickly as *I could.*'

'And since you haven't had any for twenty years I bought a bottle for you, *too.*'

45 Here are twenty pairs of words which end with the same letters but which do not rhyme. Can you say them in the correct way?

    1 pork – work   11 speak – break
    2 don – won   12 clear – pear
    3 ass – pass   13 blood – good
    4 fury – bury   14 horse – worse
    5 cost – post   15 heard – beard
    6 monkey – donkey   16 father – bather
    7 ponder – wonder   17 sorry – worry
    8 finger – singer   18 youth – south
    9 belong – among   19 sweat – heat
   10 passed – gassed   20 wallet – ballet

46 Add suitable question tags to these twenty sentences in order to form either *Yes*-expectation questions or *No*-expectation questions.

EXAMPLE 1   You'll be coming home soon, ...?
ANSWER   You'll be coming home soon, won't you?
EXAMPLE 2   He didn't want it, ...?
ANSWER   He didn't want it, did he?

  1 It's been a really lovely holiday ....?

  2 That girl certainly knows how to ski, ...?

  3 You hadn't met Nicholas before, ...?

  4 They had another garage added to their house last year, ...?

5 Mummy didn't sleep very well, ...?
6 I'm going to be unlucky again, ...?
7 Joe used to be a lot fatter than he is now, ...?
8 There's no hope of my getting that job, ...?
9 One never really knows what these politicians are going to do next, ...?
10 Ethel had her fourth child last month, ...?
11 You really shouldn't have done that, ...?
12 The Chinese invented the art of printing, ...?
13 I haven't really got to do all this again, ...?
14 Violet has a swim in the lake every morning in summer, ...?
15 That was hardly the wisest thing to do, ...?
16 Jacqueline has such a sweet smile, ...?
17 Norma'd much rather go with Keith, ...?
18 You'd better not go out tonight, with such a cold, ...?
19 I really have to have this wretched tooth out, ...?
20 He was scarcely their best President, ...?

47 The numbered blank spaces in this passage are each followed by three words in parentheses. In some cases all three of these words could be used to fill the blank spaces; in other cases, only two could be used; in other cases, only one. Make your choice now.

One day recently, I .... 1 (happened / occurred / chanced) to meet an old friend of mine, a .... 2 (resigned / retired / departed) surgeon, just coming out of a travel .... 3 (agency / office / bureau) with a .... 4 (bundle / bunch / bouquet) of .... 5 (glossy / glistening / shiny) holiday .... 6 (brochures / volumes / pamphlets) under his arm. I knew that for .... 7 (over / more / upwards) a decade he had .... 8 (passed / enjoyed / spent) a fortnight every summer at the same isolated Mediterranean village, where he had .... 9 (been / had / given) great pleasure in the warm sunshine and excellent bathing. As he was an enthusiastic motorist, he had always organised his own travelling arrangements, in a characteristically .... 10 (careful / tired / thorough) and clever manner, ... 11 (varying / changing / rotating) the routes every year. This system had enabled him to build up the most amazing collection of coloured slides, which he occasionally .... 12 (showed / performed / presented), of castles and cathedrals and notable architectural and scenic gems, all quite remote from the .... 13 (average / usual / normal) tourist itinerary. But this year, because of the .... 14 (small / minute / miniature) foreign currency allowance he was .... 15 (allowed / let / permitted) to take abroad, he had decided on an all-in package tour. The return flight, his hotel accommodation and his .... 16 (meals / food / kitchen) would .... 17 (all / both / each) be provided at an inclusive .... 18 (charge / fee / cost). Oddly enough, he was .... 19 (looking / seeing / watching) forward to this change from his .... 20 (earlier / former / previous) habits with as much eager anticipation as a child.

48 Making whatever other changes are necessary, rephrase these sentences by replacing the word *necessary* with the verb *have to* in an appropriate tense or form.

EXAMPLE 1   It may be necessary for me to do this again.
ANSWER   I *may have to* do this again.

EXAMPLE 2   It was not necessary for Caroline to take a taxi.
ANSWER   Caroline *did not have to* take a taxi.

1 It might be necessary for us to buy new tyres for the car.
2 It has been necessary for Sandra to break off her engagement.
3 It was necessary for our parents to leave earlier than usual.
4 It will be necessary for this tooth to be taken out.
5 It used to be necessary for us to sleep under mosquito nets.
6 We are sorry to announce that it has been necessary for the Minister to resign from the Cabinet.
7 It will certainly be necessary for the landlord to pay for this repair.
8 They were disappointed because it had been necessary for them to miss our wedding.
9 It could be necessary for the Mayor to abandon his plans.
10 I was sorry about the damage I caused, but it was necessary for me to break the lock on the suitcase.
11 If your cheque hadn't arrived when it did, it would have been necessary for us to ask someone to lend us some money.
12 It is going to be necessary for me to lose some weight if I want to wear these trousers comfortably.
13 Since you forgot to buy bread, it will be necessary for the whole family to be as economical as possible with what we have left.
14 It is not necessary for you to wait here. Please come inside.
15 Why was it necessary for Gerard to have the whole of his head shaved?

49 For your convenience, this passage has been divided into three sections. Carefully read each section twice, and then answer the questions that follow it.

Section 1

My parents were hardly seated in the Brimlows' kitchen, and my father was still wondering how to open the unpleasant business, when the sound of the front door was heard. Luther was not alone. He came into the kitchen pale and trembling,
5 and with him was a tall, well-dressed man who looked in a thoroughly black humour. Luther licked his lips and explained that this was Mr Armroyd, the stockbroker who employed him. Mr Armroyd began without preliminary: 'I'm saving the police a job by bringing your son along myself, Mr Brimlow.'
10 Luther immediately began to babble: 'I can explain everything, Mother. It's all a mistake. It wasn't stealing. It was nothing but borrowing.'
It was at once to his mother that he appealed. Poor old Brimlow from the start was hardly in the picture. Mrs Brimlow
15 did not lose her self-possession. Her narrow cunning face sharpened, and she said, 'I think your husband ought to leave us, Mrs Pentecost. And you, too.'
My father answered her sharply. 'I'm not so sure about that, Mrs Brimlow.' And, turning to Mr Armroyd, he added: 'My
20 wife and I – we live next door – we've just come in here to settle some matters that concern this young man. They may be related to what you have to say, and if we have your permission we shall stay.'
Mrs Brimlow, sniffing danger like a vixen, cried, 'I won't
25 have it! This is my house, and who stays in it is my business – not Mr Armroyd's or anyone else's.'
Mr Armroyd said in a sharp, reminding voice, 'Mrs Brimlow, I told you that I had brought your son along rather than allow the police to do it. If you are unreasonable, I shall have to
30 change my mind. Then it won't be a question of your next-door neighbour knowing what has happened, but of everybody knowing it.'

1 In line 31, Mr Armroyd speaks of 'what has happened'. Find the single word in this section that explains what in fact had happened.

2 Find three words or phrases that show that Luther was afraid.

3 What does *in the picture* (line 14) mean?

4 Explain the meaning of *hardly* in

   a *hardly seated* (line 1);
   b *hardly in the picture* (line 14).

5 In what two ways does the author compare Mrs Brimlow to a fox?

6 What danger did Mrs Brimlow sniff (line 24)?

7 Which two possible meanings could be understood from:

   a *My wife and I have just come in here to settle some matters that concern this young man* (lines 19–21)?
   b *They may be related to what you have to say* (line 21)?

Section 2

Mrs Brimlow was one of those fools who never see reason. 'You can say what you like,' she shouted. 'I won't believe a word of it. Our Luther's a good boy, and a hard-working boy, and a clever boy. What about your own letters? Haven't you written to say how good he was, more than once?'

Mr Armroyd's eyebrows shot up, and Luther said suddenly, 'Oh, leave it alone, Mother. You'll do no good.' But already Mrs Brimlow was searching in a sideboard drawer, and she brought out three letters headed with the name of Mr Armroyd's firm. Luther made a snatch for them, but Mr Armroyd managed to take them first. He gave a glance at all three, folded them carefully, and put them in his pocket. 'These interest me enormously,' he said. 'It seems to me, Mrs Brimlow, that your son will go far – in one direction or another. Stealing from the petty-cash box is common enough with boys of his sort and at his age, but such a neat bit of forgery is not usual.'

He looked with renewed interest at Luther, who was now white and shaking. 'Are you such a poor specimen,' he asked, 'that you must bolster yourself up like this even to your own parents?'

There could be no doubt now, even in Mrs Brimlow's mind.
55 She put her arms round her son and shrieked at Mr Armroyd, 'You leave him alone! You slave-driver! Is it any wonder that the poor boy steals when you pay him a wage I'd be ashamed to give to a washerwoman?'

8 Why did Mr Armroyd's eyebrows shoot up (line 38)?

9 Why did Luther make a snatch for the letters?

10 Why did Mr Armroyd put the letters in his pocket?

11 What further information are we given in this section about the crime that Luther was suspected of in the first section?

12 What did Mr Armroyd mean when he told Mrs Brimlow that her son would go far – in one direction or another (line 46)?

13 When he spoke to Luther, what did he mean by **a** *a poor specimen* (line 51) and **b** *bolster yourself up* (line 52)?

14 Which word in particular shows that Luther was still afraid?

15 *There could be no doubt now* (line 54). What of?

16 Put into reported speech:
   a Mrs Brimlow's words in lines 34–37
   b Luther's words in lines 38–39
   c Mr Armroyd's words in lines 44–49
   d Mr Armroyd's words in lines 51–53
   e Mrs Brimlow's words in lines 55–58

Section 3

Mr Armroyd interrupted her. 'Mrs Brimlow, I came here to
tell you that for a long time your son has been stealing
considerable sums of money. I have learned from you that he
is also a forger. Now listen to me, if you can stop your tongue
clacking for a moment. I'm surprised that one or two things
have not struck you. Your son dresses expensively for his
situation. He travels first class on the railway. I've seen him at
lunchtime in rather expensive restaurants entertaining a young
lady. This young man has got to be cleared out of Manchester.
He's flying a bit too high, even though I recently raised his
salary to a rate higher than is usually paid. But I imagine he
hasn't told you that. However, I did it, and I'll tell you why.'

He slapped the pocket containing the forged letters.

'If I *had* written those letters they would have said just about
what your son said about himself. He has shown exceptional
cleverness in my business. He could have gone a long way with
clean hands. But in my office he's not going any way at all with
dirty hands. Nor anywhere else in Manchester, so far as I can
prevent it.'

17 Find the words that most clearly show that:
   a Luther was guilty of more than one theft.
   b Mr Armroyd's loss had not been light.
   c Mr Armroyd found that Mrs Brimlow's voice was unpleasant.
   d Luther's tastes were not in keeping with his salary.
   e Luther might have had a very successful career.

18 What is the meaning of *struck* in line 64?

19 What did Mr Armroyd mean when he spoke of clean hands and dirty hands?

On the whole passage

20 In what way had Mr Armroyd shown a very considerate attitude towards his employee?

50 Rephrase each of these sentences in such a way that you can use the word that appears in capital letters. Do not alter this word in any way.

EXAMPLE   I suppose they are all away for the weekend. MUST
ANSWER   They must all be away for the weekend.

1 I'm not going to retire until I myself want to. FEEL

2 That hotel is a bit too expensive for us, I'm afraid. REACH

3 I don't personally care if they come or not. MATTER

4 After two hours the bridegroom had still not arrived. SIGN

5 We didn't go to the island that stormy weekend in case we couldn't get back. FEAR

6 Rosalind found the heat and humidity quite intolerable. BEAR

7 It's going to pour. I think you should take a mackintosh. HAD

8 Many of the group had not been in a helicopter before. TIME

9 Yes, it's a great pity my father was so absent-minded last night. WISH

10 I don't think Geoffrey will be able to do that job. CAPABLE

11 You shouldn't pay so much attention to their complaints. NOTICE

12 We insist on knowing the truth about all this. DEMAND

13 Everybody enjoyed the play except Raymond. ONLY

14 It's such a large house that she doesn't like being alone in it. OWN

15 Go and ask Winifred. I'm sure she'll know the answer. BOUND

16 Who gave you my name and address? TOUCH

17 All of a sudden, Alice thought of a solution to the problem. OCCURRED

18 It is very interesting to talk to him. HE

19 Your hair is much too long, dear. NEEDS

20 This is the last time I ask you to help me. NEVER

51 Here are twenty adjectives arranged in alphabetical order. Rearrange them in five groups, bringing together those which are similar or related in meaning. Each group should have four adjectives.

affluent	competent	experienced	peaceful	timid
anxious	deceitful	frightened	quiet	untrue
calm	deceptive	misleading	relaxed	wealthy
capable	efficient	nervous	rich	well-to-do

52 In English, there are about sixty idiomatic comparisons like *as mad as a hatter* (meaning extremely mad) and *as poor as a church mouse* (meaning extremely poor).

Can you fill in the missing words in these twenty?

1 as deaf as a ....
2 as fresh as a ....
3 as sound as a ....
4 as hungry as a ....
5 as light as a ....
6 as mischievous as a ....
7 as obstinate as a ....
8 as old as the ....
9 as quiet as a ....
10 as sweet as ....
11 as .... as a lion.
12 as .... as a whistle.
13 as .... as ice.
14 as .... as a berry.
15 as .... as a poker.
16 as .... as a picture.
17 as .... as a peacock.
18 as .... as an eel.
19 as .... as a bat.
20 as .... as an ox.

53 If we say *We are going to build a new garage,* we mean that we are going to build it ourselves. If, however, we are going to pay or ask someone else to build it for us, we normally use the causative construction of the verb *have: We are going to have a new garage built.*

Rephrase each of these sentences with this causative construction.

EXAMPLE   Daphne made a couple of dresses last week.
ANSWER   Daphne *had a couple of dresses made* last week.

1 Shall we cut down this tree?

2 Noel serviced his car thoroughly before he started on the long journey.

3 Why didn't you sharpen all these knives as you said you would?

4 I ought to put a light outside the front door.

5 The Jenkinsons haven't yet put a fireplace in their cottage as they said they would.

6 We have to polish these floors at least once a month.

7 The law says that everyone must put seat-belts on the front seats at least.

8 Fred doesn't clean his shoes on the way to work any longer.

9 I must either buy a new typewriter or repair this one.

10 Let's dye these curtains red. They'll look much better.

11 One shouldn't forget to check the pressure of one's tyres from time to time.

12 My sister has made a lovely dress out of a discarded parachute that her boyfriend gave her.

13 We had to lift the car on to a breakdown truck after the accident.

14 The Whittomes are building a swimming pool in their garden.

15 Madge and Cyril didn't have enough money to put a new roof on the house last year. They are putting it on now.

54 Finish each of the incomplete sentences below in such a way that it has the same meaning as the sentence which is printed above it.

EXAMPLE   It would be wise for us to take raincoats.
We'd ....
ANSWER   We'd better take raincoats.

1. Whoever did that must have been a very brave person.
Only ....

2. Doris tiptoed up the stairs because she didn't want to wake anyone up.
For fear ....

3. 'Why didn't you invite us too?' she said reproachfully.
She said: 'You might ....'

4. Nancy is proud of being a good cook.
Nancy prides ....

5. My protests were ignored by everybody.
Nobody ....

6. I'm sure it was by mistake that he took your umbrella.
I'm sure he didn't ....

7. We'll arrive soon – and then we'll all be able to have a beer.
Once ....

8. Katherine is the only real friend that Dolly has.
Except ....

9. It's a great pity you wrote that letter.
I wish ....

10. Ralph's passport was nowhere to be found.
Nobody ....

11. The last time we were here was in 1980.
We ....

12. Rita doesn't realise how serious her husband's operation is going to be.
Little ....

13. He decided to repair the thing himself and not to take it back to the shop.
Rather ....

14 'Please don't drive so fast!' Kathleen begged her boyfriend.
Kathleen pleaded ....

15 Offering her more money wouldn't make any difference.
Even if ....

16 But for Ivor's help we would have been in serious trouble.
If ....

17 Driving at that speed is dangerous on this road, whether you are an experienced driver or not, Sir.
However ....

18 Your hair really needs cutting, doesn't it, Paddy?
Your hair really must ....

19 It's such a wonderful opportunity that we mustn't miss it.
It's too ....

20 Paul left the room without saying a word.
Paul didn't ....

55 Here are ten sentences, each followed by three suggested explanations. Only one of the explanations is correct. Can you say which it is?

1 Wait a moment! It's on the tip of my tongue.
  a Something is hurting my tongue.
  b I can't speak for the moment.
  c I shall remember it in a moment.

2 The Jacksons are terribly hard up.
  a They live a very long way up the hill.
  b They are extremely poor.
  c They are cruel people.

3 Dr Naylor is practising somewhere in the Scottish highlands now.
  a He is treating patients there now.
  b It is there that he is taking mountaineering practice now.
  c He is still studying medicine somewhere in the highlands.

4 Go and see what the children are up to.
  a I want to know if they need anything.
  b I want to know what mischievous things they are doing.
  c I want to know which tree they have climbed this time.

5 I'll lay my cards on the table.
  a I want to stop playing.
  b I'll be back in a moment or two.
  c I'll have no secrets from you.

6 That will put the cat among the pigeons!
  a That will cause a lot of trouble.
  b The cat will have to stay outside the house tonight.
  c Then we shall have as many cats as we have pigeons.

7 We're going to get into hot water when we arrive home.
  a We're going to have a nice hot bath.
  b We're going to have trouble.
  c The water will have become hot by then.

8 The boss is like a bear with a sore head today.
  a He has a very bad headache.
  b He is in a bad mood.
  c He badly needs a haircut.

9 What's happened? You look as if you've been in the wars.
  a You look like an old soldier.
  b You are wearing a lot of medals.
  c You look as though something unpleasant has happened to you.

10 My fingers are all thumbs!
  a I am extremely clumsy.
  b My fingers are all very thick.
  c I am trying to attract your attention.

56 The word in capital letters at the end of each of these sentences can be changed in such a way that it forms a word that fits suitably in the blank space. Fill each blank in this way.

EXAMPLE   The bloodstain on her dress was very .... NOTICE

ANSWER   The bloodstain on her dress was very *noticeable*.

1 The hurricane caused terrible .... along the coast. DESTROY

2 I have never worked for such a considerate .... I think all the other .... have the same opinion. EMPLOY

3 Without your .... he would never have been able to do it. COURAGE

4 I feel so .... that I'm going to bed. SLEEP

5 The cost of .... must be paid by the buyer. CARRY

6 I'm sure we can believe her. She's usually very .... TRUTH

7 He is .... of what he has done. SHAME

8 A successful business needs good .... ORGANISE

9 The ring was not at all valuable; in fact, it was almost .... WORTH

10 You must realise that such .... cannot be tolerated. OBEY

11 Jenny has sent me a very .... letter explaining why she didn't do what she promised. APOLOGY

12 Scientists are beginning to believe that the .... of the planets next century is not impossible. COLONY

13 Let's go for a picnic tomorrow unless the weather forecast is .... FAVOUR

14 Don't put on any more of that perfume, Julie. It's .... stuff. HEAD

15 Your job will be to see that no .... product leaves this part of the factory. PERFECT

16 Sheila says she feels .... and fed up. She needs a holiday. WEAR

17 The floor of the attic needs .... if we're going to make it into a bedroom. STRONG

18 The number of .... in the factory has increased so much that the police have been asked to investigate. THIEF

19 Thanks to your .... we have now collected the money we need. GENEROUS

20 I'm afraid there is going to be another .... of the currency soon. VALUE

57 Make all the changes and additions necessary to produce, from the following ten groups of words and phrases, a complete letter from Ofeyi Obote to the Principal of Stanhope College in London. (See Exercise 7 for an example, if necessary.)

Dear Sir,
I / be / present / student / final year / City High School / Harare / Zimbabwe.

1 ....

I / Study / English / five years / now

2 ....

June / this year / sit / First Certificate examination / University of Cambridge / hope / pass / good grade

3 ....
....

Also / expect / obtain / High School Certificate / about / same time / high marks / particularly / biology

4 ....
....

Ambition / enter / London University / due course / read for / degree / genetics

5 ....

Realise / necessary / G.C.E. / qualify / entrance / university

6 ....

Very much hope / accepted / your College / prepare / G.C.E. / Chemistry / Biology / English too

7 ....
....

Would like / start / early autumn / not / waste time

8 ....

Perhaps / add father and mother / both / doctors / so / brought up / scientific environment

9 ....

Grateful / you send / official application form / and inform / other information / required

10 ....

Yours faithfully, *Ofeyi Obote*

58 Fill each of the numbered blank spaces in this passage with ONE suitable word.

Hadley was in a bad .... 1 when he joined his friends in the bar of the Hilton Hotel. 'A large whisky and soda, please,' he said to the waiter who .... 2 him as he sat down. He put his head in his hands. 'Oh my God!' he said.

'What's the .... 3?' asked Chalkey.

Hadley breathed heavily a .... 4 of times before replying. 'The inefficiency of this country!' he said. 'Never in all my life have I seen anything .... 5 it.'

'What's happened?'

'What *hasn't* happened! I've been here .... 6 only eight days and fourteen things have gone wrong.'

'You get .... 7 to it,' said Blake. 'I've been here for twenty years and things have been going wrong for me all the time. But they're charming people.'

'Oh yes,' said Hadley. 'They're very charming, I'll .... 8 you that. But how the country survives is something beyond my .... 9. And how you .... 10 up with it I'll never understand. The .... 11 I finish my job of work and get .... 12 the better. I'll go off my .... 13 otherwise.'

'What has .... 14 you this afternoon?'

'I have .... 15 come from a dry-cleaner's,' said Hadley. 'It is said to be a reliable one. Six days ago, I took a light-grey suit to be cleaned. It .... 16 promised for the following day, at a certain time. I went there at the time, and every day after that. The suit was .... 17 given to me half an hour ago. And do you know what they have .... 18 to it?'

'I can think of a good many things,' said Chalkey. 'But what?'

'They have dyed it navy blue.' Hadley took a long drink from his glass.

.... 19 the laughter, Blake asked: 'What was their excuse? They're good at excuses.'

'They didn't make an excuse,' said Hadley. 'They smiled very sweetly and said that navy blue will .... 20 me much better than grey.'

87

59 Fill the blank spaces in these sentences with the appropriate tense (either active or passive) of the verb which appears in capital letters on the right.

EXAMPLE I .... that film twice, so I don't want to see it again. SEE

ANSWER have seen

1 Gertrude .... a new car last week. BUY

2 Joseph .... in that flat for at least six months now. LIVE

3 I .... my watch. Do tell me, please, if you see it anywhere. LOSE

4 It's high time you .... the car. WASH

5 Sean .... from Dublin and has a charming Irish accent. COME

6 It's getting late. It's time we .... home. GO

7 If we hadn't been able to get seats for the play, we .... very disappointed. BE

8 Will you please give him this message the moment he .... ARRIVE

9 This is the second time that I .... this film. SEE

10 If I .... Prime Minister, I would be very unhappy about that. BE

11 I hope it will rain soon. We .... a drop for nearly a month. NOT HAVE

12 Guy .... for a job since he left university. LOOK

13 We would have lent you the money if we .... that you were in such difficulty. KNOW

14 The Glovers .... dinner when the wind took the roof of their house off. HAVE

15 On the seventh of next month we .... married for exactly ten years. BE

16 My brother left yesterday for Freiburg. He .... to give a lecture in the university there. INVITE

17 Angus .... for his company for twelve years when they made him a director of the Board. WORK

18 When Grannie ...., I think she will be very tired. ARRIVE

19 I wish you .... with us tomorrow. COME

20 We'd better not wait any longer for him. I expect he .... all about this meeting this morning. FORGET

60 Choose from the four phrases in *italics* after each of the following sentences the one which most suitably fills the blank spaces.

1 What Father said was brief and ....
on the point   to the point   up to a point   in point

2 Yes, we do eat out ...., but not very often. It's so expensive nowadays.
in time   from time to time   against time   at one time

3 We didn't much like the new neighbours at first, but .... we grew quite fond of them.
by the time   in time   at the same time   against time

4 You might be able to get their flat if you're lucky. They're .... of giving it up.
beside the point   to the point   on the point   in point

5 ...., his secretary wears the most extraordinary clothes.
With time   At one time   At times   In time

6 We're fighting .... to finish the job for you before the end of the week.
in time   on time   by the time   against time

7 I don't think you understand what I mean about the stupidity of the new law. Well, here is a case ....
to the point   beside the point   in point   on the point

8 .... the fire brigade found our mountain house, we had put out the fire ourselves with the garden hosepipe.
With time   By the time   At the same time   In time

9 They're most unpunctual people but because the boss was going to be at the party they had to be .... for once.
in time   to time   with time   at the same time

10 You're talking nonsense, Jack. What you have just said is quite ....
up to a point   beside the point   in point   on the point

11 You're quite right, of course, but .... you needn't have been so rude about it.
at one time   from time to time   at the same time   at times

12 We were allowed .... to park our car outside our front door.
by the time   in time   with time   at one time

13 I agree with you .... but there are some other things to consider, too.
up to a point   to the point   beside the point   in point

14 I'm sure that when it comes .... she won't marry him, after all.
in point   up to a point   to the point   in point

15 It's wonderful! The trains here always leave, and nearly always arrive ....
in time   on time   to time   with time

61 In each of these sentences replace the phrase that is printed in *italics* with a phrase of similar meaning containing the preposition **of**. You may need to make changes to some words or to add articles like **a**, **the**, etc., but you must not make further changes.

EXAMPLE   *Children's portraits* are difficult to paint.
ANSWER   The portraits of children are difficult to paint.

1 Mona has been *a stamp collector* for many years.
2 Leo has an *egg-shaped head*.
3 *His life-story* is very interesting.
4 Nuffield makes his living now by writing *film reviews*.
5 The Pattersons have *solid marble steps* leading up to their front door.

6 I've always been entranced by *Shakespearian sonnets*.

7 We suffer awfully from *aircraft-noise* in this village.

8 I have been *Club Secretary* for the last six years.

9 Every worker in the factory has to be a *union member*.

10 It will be a *one-and-a-half-hour lecture*.

11 An extra tax has been imposed on *helicopter-owners*.

12 *Music-lovers* will be delighted with this news.

13 You seem to have developed a *mulish obstinacy*.

14 Laura has just bought *an expensive rubberised-silk mackintosh*.

15 In his youth, Harris won an Olympic medal for *weight-lifting*.

16 You can hear everything they say in the next room. It is only *a cardboard wall* between us.

17 This is *an eighteen-carat gold bracelet*.

18 Ursula says it's romantic to have dinner by *candlelight*.

19 Is that *a book-cover* that's lying on the floor?

20 *Road-making* is my company's principal work these days.

62 Here are twenty sentences each with a blank space. Below each one are four words or phrases. Choose which one of these most suitably fills the blank space.

1. I wish you wouldn't .... your clothes all over the floor.
   stray   sprawl   scatter   straggle

2. Little Angela hasn't .... her shyness yet.
   got over   got away from   got through   got under

3. They all take too much .... of his kindness and generosity.
   profit   advantage   benefit   use

4. Father would not .... us to go there for the weekend.
   let   permit   agree   consent

5. You can trust what he says. He's a very .... person.
   reliable   trustful   profitable   depending

6. Aunt Ida has never really .... from her nervous breakdown.
   mended   cured   recovered   repaired

7. Diana .... over a stone and fell flat on her face.
   dripped   tripped   stepped   walked

8. Steak for breakfast and eggs for supper is ...., to say the least.
   erratic   eccentric   egocentric   egoistic

9. Much stricter .... must now be taken at all airports.
   precautions   alarms   warnings   protections

10. Many countries still rely on rice as the .... food.
    capital   staple   superior   winning

11. Inflation and its upward .... is the scourge of our days.
    trend   bend   stream   move

12. The United States .... from voting at the United Nations yesterday.
    discontinued   refused   rejected   abstained

13. The main .... of this drink are wine, orange juice and bitters.
    parts   components   compositions   ingredients

14 I'm so out of .... that I can't run ten metres without puffing.
    health   strength   condition   fitness

15 All traffic is being .... because of the military parades.
    diverted   converted   changed   altered

16 I'm afraid Grandfather's writing is becoming more and more ....
    illegible   illiterate   eligible   incoherent

17 Your progress will be .... in six months' time.
    counted   evaluated   valued   enumerated

18 The main .... to progress is not technical but political.
    prevention   obstacle   clash   reverse

19 This .... invention of yours should make you rich.
    genial   talented   genius   ingenious

20 The .... of these volunteers for hard work is amazing.
    ability   capacity   capability   efficiency

63

In English, there are seven different ways in which the letters *-ough* are pronounced at the end of the word. Here are twelve words ending in *-ough*. Can you say how each is pronounced?

1 borough	4 dough	7 rough	10 through
2 bough	5 hiccough	8 thorough	11 tough
3 cough	6 plough	9 though	12 trough

64 Change the infinitives in brackets into either the (active or passive) Past Simple or the Present Perfect, according to what is required in English usage.

1 What a nuisance! I (forget) my keys again!

2 When we first (come) to this town, it (be) relatively easy to find a parking place near our house. Now it (become) a big problem.

3 Midnight – and my husband (not arrive) home and (not telephone)! I'm beginning to be very worried. He (say) this morning that he would be home for dinner as usual.

4 We're lucky to have Jackson. He is the best Maths teacher this school ever (have).

5 Do you remember the drive we (take) through the Loire valley five or six years ago? I think we (take) a lot of photographs, but I can't find them. I (look) in the album but there's nothing there. Have you any idea where they (put)?

6 A hole (appear) in each elbow of this jacket. I (buy) some leather patches on the way home yesterday. Could you sew them on for me, please?

7 Oh, hello, Miss Richards. How nice that you (come) to our party. A lot of people (ask) whether you were coming. They all (say) they want to meet you.

8 There (be) a terrific uproar in Parliament yesterday. Many Members (be) very angry about the answer the Prime Minister (give) to a question. The P.M. (say), however, that she (not be) in the least surprised or disturbed.

9 I (finish) this work at last, thank God! I (not expect) that it would be so difficult.

10 They (start) to build this motorway three years ago, and they still (not finish) it!

11 We (go) to the Rex Cinema last Saturday. What a stupid film it (be)! We (waste) both our time and our money. I'd like to know something about the film that is there this week. Any of you (see) it?

12 You (ask) whether we're going to that lecture. We don't know. In any case, we (not receive) an invitation.

13 Don't be surprised when you see how thin Olaf is. He (be) extremely ill.

14 Neil's first book (be) very successful and (sell) nearly a hundred thousand copies before it (go) out of print. His second book is still doing well and already (sell) almost as many.

15 The man who (escape) last night from Dartmoor Prison (capture). He (shoot) two guards dead as he (make) his get-away, and (wound) two others at the time he (capture). It is suspected that the gun he (use) (bring) to him by a recent visitor.

65 Here are twenty verbs arranged in alphabetical order. Rearrange them in five groups, bringing together those which are similar or related in meaning. Each group should have four verbs.

attach	fasten	march	save	tap
bang	fix	ransom	secure	tramp
beat	knock	rap	spank	thrash
cane	liberate	rescue	stroll	wander

66 Fill each of these blank spaces with a suitable word or phrase of your choice.

EXAMPLE Two convicts are reported .... from the prison last night.
ANSWER to have escaped *or* to have got away.

1 If only .... with us. It wasn't any fun at all without you.

2 Wherever have you been? We .... for you everywhere.

3 Why do .... on asking the same question? I've told you I'm not going to answer.

4 If you had been in my place, what .... taken?

5 After he .... there for a few weeks, Owen will settle down in his new school.

6 You'd .... him exactly what happened. He'll find out from somebody else if you don't.

7 I don't like cheese for breakfast, and .... my wife.

8 The Richardsons have a twelve .... house, so they are able to invite lots of guests.

9 I wish you .... telling that joke, Oscar. Everybody has heard it too often.

10 It's a lovely evening. Let's go out for a walk, ...?

11 You started on the problem only half an hour ago. Surely .... it up already?

12 There's a fair .... food left over from the party. We'll have it tomorrow.

13 Madeleine is .... you could ever hope to meet.

14 I've warned you not to disturb that dog, Rodney. If you get bitten, it .... fault.

15 The sheriff kicked open the door and entered the saloon, a gun in each hand. 'All of you put .... air!' he said to the men at the bar.

16 If .... answered their letter, it would have been very rude of us.

17 I don't know how to mend this two-way switch. It .... by an electrician.

18 You didn't have to come all the way by bus. We .... station in the car to pick you up.

19 The Mercedes overtook us at a very high speed. It must .... more than 180 k.p.h.

20 Kitty says she's not used .... bed as early as this in her own home.

67 Fill in the blank space in each of the sentences below with an appropriate modal (must, would, should, etc.).

1. Patrick has a yacht and a helicopter. He .... be extremely rich.
2. We waited for over an hour for you. You really .... have telephoned to say you were not coming.
3. Why didn't you do it? You promised you ...., for certain.
4. Mother is awfully lonely now. We .... spend more time with her.
5. They left only an hour ago. They .... hardly have arrived yet.
6. There's a chance that he'll arrive in time for supper, but he .... be a lot later.
7. Neil ate all the food so hungrily and quickly that he .... have been a wolf.
8. We should all wash our hands before putting them in our mouths, but dentists absolutely ....
9. Eat whatever you .... We'll put the rest in the fridge and have it for lunch tomorrow.
10. We .... meet there every Sunday, until they closed the place down.
11. Have you heard about all the things that happened? It can't have been a very pleasant holiday for them, ... it?
12. I can't see my umbrella anywhere. I .... have left it in the office.
13. You can hear so much of what is going on in the next rooms that the walls of that hotel .... be made of cardboard.
14. She .... always do it before anyone asked her to.
15. I'm so sleepy that I .... scarcely keep my eyes open.

68 Here are some sentences with verbs in the passive voice. Making whatever other changes are necessary, rephrase the sentences with the verbs in the active voice.

EXAMPLE Your car *is being brought* now, Sir.
ANSWER   Somebody is *bringing* your car now, Sir.

1 Has all that been understood by all of you?
2 Weren't you informed that there is going to be a meeting?
3 The chair had to be thrown away because its springs had been broken.
4 My father wants to resign but he has been asked to stay on for another year or so. His presence on the Board is said to be valuable.
5 Was the medal given by the Queen herself?
6 A new stretch of motorway is going to be built between Graz and Lund.
7 Politics are seen by many ambitious men as a stepping-stone to power.
8 A window had been smashed and everything that was in the car had been stolen.
9 The meanings of these words are often confused.
10 Are those funny hats worn by all their policemen?
11 Antibiotics are wrongly believed by some people to be the cure for a common cold.
12 Who was this written by? I insist on being told the truth.
13 At last we have been invited to one of their receptions.
14 The one-time storeroom above the garage is being turned into a spare bedroom.
15 You are allowed to go there only if you are a Moslem.
16 The policeman's attention was suddenly caught by a small box which had been placed under the Minister's car.
17 Maurice was summoned by the manager, strongly reprimanded, and threatened with immediate dismissal if the same thing was ever done again.

18 The burning question that this Government is faced with is what can be done about unemployment.

19 During the month that he was held prisoner by the terrorists, the General was chained to his bed for twenty-three-and-a-half-hours out of twenty-four. And he was not allowed ever to see their faces or hear their voices.

20 Very well, Sir. Your car shall be given our 'B' Service this morning. It shall be washed and polished this afternoon, and returned to you at five o'clock.

69

One of the nine particles shown below can be used *after* each of the verbs in these sentences to form a noun. Say which one is needed in each case.

between   by   down   in   off   out   over   through   up

EXAMPLE When you travel on the buses in this city, be on the look .... for pickpockets.
ANSWER   look*out*

1 Nothing was decided, I'm afraid. The meeting was a complete wash ....

2 Hurry, Madam! Boarding for your flight has already finished. Take .... will be in about fifteen minutes.

3 The most urgently needed medical break .... today is a cure for AIDS.

4 At night this square is filled with hundreds of punks and drop ....

5 Miller is hoping to be elected a Member of Parliament in the next election but, with such strong opposition, I don't think he'll have a look- ....

6 I'm getting very angry with the people above us about their late-night parties every two or three days. It's time we had a show ....

7 We keep this old electric fire as a stand .... in case we ever have a break .... of our central heating system.

8 There'll be some left .... from the party, I expect. If there are, we'll have them for supper tomorrow.

9 An accident on the main road into town has caused an awful hold .... of traffic.

10 Have you heard about the break .... of Ted and Myrna's marriage?

11 The company uses Les Davidson as a go- .... when the management and the trade union are having one of their disputes.

12 These two companies deny that there is any sort of tie- .... between them, but I think there is.

13 Did you see on TV last night the tremendous send- .... the Queen was given as she left for the States?

14 In spite of the recession, the firm's turn .... last year was not at all bad.

15 The police are still searching for three escaped convicts after the break .... from Dartmoor Prison last week.

70 In spoken English, one syllable of the words in *italics* below would be given strong stress. Can you say which one?

EXAMPLE I *adore* you, Lulu!
ANSWER   ad*ore*

1 We were *entirely enveloped* by the fog.

2 With his good looks and all that money, he's an *extremely eligible* young *bachelor*.

3 If you'd allow me to do so, I'd like to *record* the *discussion*.

4 Unfortunately, many people throw their *refuse* into the *canal*.

5 No, it's the other way round! Things *expand* in the heat and *contract* in the cold.

6 Everything was all right at the end but there were some *irritating upsets* at the beginning.

7 The *correspondents* were *subjected* to a lot of rudeness at the *frontier*.

8 The differences between this new *contract* and the old one are *minute*.

9 Here is the *extract* that you wanted from that article on *injuries*.

10 It says that the job carries both *executive* and *administrative responsibilities*. I wonder what the difference is?

71 Carefully read the following passage twice, and then answer the questions.

However much one groaned about it beforehand, however much one hated arranging decorations and doing up parcels and ordering several days' meals in advance, when it actually came Christmas Day was always fun.
5 It began in the same way every year: the handle of Mrs Miniver's bedroom door being turned just loudly enough to wake her up, but not so loudly as to count as waking her up on purpose; Toby in the dark doorway, clutching in one hand a pillow-case filled with Christmas presents and toys, and holding
10 up his pyjama trousers with the other.
'Toby! It's only six o'clock!'
'But, Mummy, I can't tell the time.' He was barefoot and shivering, and his eyes were like stars.
'Oh, all right. Come and get warm, you little goat.' He was
15 in her bed like a flash, toys and all. The tail of a clockwork dog scratched her back.
A few minutes later, another head round the door, a little higher up.
'But Judy darling, it's *too* early. Honestly!'
20 'I know, but I heard Toby come in, so I knew you must be awake.'
'All right, you can come into bed, too, but you simply must keep quiet. Daddy's still asleep, though I can't imagine how he can be.'
25 And then a third head, higher up still, and Vin's deeper voice. 'I say, are the others in here? I thought I heard them.'
By that time, of course, Mr Miniver was awake, too. The old transparent plan had worked perfectly once more. There was

nothing for it but to shut the windows, switch on the lights, and
30 admit that Christmas Day had begun.
   The three right hands – Vin's strong and broad, Judy's thin
and flexible, Toby's still a starfish – plunged in and out of the
three pillow-cases until they were empty. Their methods were
as different as their hands. Vin examined each object carefully
35 before he went on to the next. Judy, talking the whole time,
pulled all her treasures out in a heap, took a quick glance at
them and went straight for the one she liked best. Toby pulled
all his out, too, but he arranged them in a neat pattern on the
bed-cover and looked at them in complete silence for a long
40 time. Then he picked up one – a big glass ball with coloured
rings in it – and put it by itself a little way off. After that he
played with the other toys, appreciatively enough, but from
time to time his eyes would stray towards the ball, as though to
make sure it was still waiting for him.
45 Mrs Miniver watched him with a mixture of delight and
misgiving. It was her own favourite approach to life. There
was a trouble, though. The ball sometimes rolled away.

   1 Why do you think meals had to be ordered in advance (line 3)?
   2 Consider the meaning of *actually* in line 3. What would be a suitable synonym for its meaning here?
   3 Why were Toby's eyes like stars as he stood in the doorway?
   4 In line 15, we have the expression *toys and all*. Does this mean *all* the toys, or do you think there is a different meaning?
   5 What connection is there between a clockwork dog and a clock?
   6 Can you think why the word *Honestly!* in line 19 appears as a separate sentence?
   7 Which sentences in the first half of the passage show a feeling of love and irritation at the same time?
   8 What, in fact, was the old transparent plan (line 27)?
   9 Why is it described as being transparent?
   10 Why does the writer use the verb *admit* in line 30?
   11 Why is Toby's hand described as a starfish (line 32)?

12 Why did Toby put his glass ball on one side?

13 In line 47, we have *The ball sometimes rolled away*. Is there a figurative meaning here? If there is, explain it in your own words.

14 What is the meaning of *misgiving* in line 46?

15 Why did Mrs Miniver feel something of misgiving as she watched Toby?

16 What are the differences in meaning of:

    a *enough* in lines 6 and 42?
    b *too* in lines 19 and 22?
    c *must* in lines 20 and 22?

17 Which of the three children appears to be the most thoughtful, and which the most impulsive?

18 Explain the meaning of:

    a *had worked perfectly* (line 28);
    b *There was nothing for it* (line 28);
    c *went straight for* (line 37);
    d *his eyes would stray* (line 43);
    e *as though to make sure* (line 43).

19 Which words or phrases are used in this passage to give the meaning of:

    a tying?
    b deliberately?
    c without shoes or slippers?
    d separately?
    e occasionally?

20 Give another word or short phrase that could be substituted for each of these without any change of meaning:

    a *groaned* (line 1)   g *transparent* (line 28)
    b *arranging* (line 2)   h *flexible* (line 32)
    c *ordering* (line 3)   i *examined* (line 34)
    d *loudly* (line 6)   j *neat* (line 38)
    e *count* (line 7)   k *complete* (line 39)
    f *clutching* (line 8)   l *stray* (line 43)

72 Say what each of these twenty things is used for by answering the imaginary question 'What's a .... for?' or 'What are .... for?'. Your answers should begin with 'It's' or 'They're' and then use an infinitive, and end with a preposition.

EXAMPLE a refrigerator (What's a refrigerator for?)
ANSWER   It's to keep food fresh in.

1 a bath	8 bandages	15 scissors
2 a calculator	9 a kitchen sink	16 a shotgun
3 a camera	10 a notebook	17 a table
4 a prison cell	11 a parachute	18 a university
5 a fireplace	12 a park	19 a video
6 a generator	13 a razor	20 a piano
7 gloves	14 a school	

73 Remove the words in *italics* in each of these sentences, and then rephrase the sentences with the verb *wish*, making whatever other changes are necessary but without changing the meaning.

EXAMPLE 1 I *am sorry* I didn't give anything to that beggar.
ANSWER   I wish I had given something to that beggar.

EXAMPLE 2 *It's a pity* we couldn't arrive earlier.
ANSWER   We wish we could have arrived earlier.
   or   We wish we had been able to arrive earlier.

1 I *am sorry* I did not go on the earlier train.

2 *It is a pity* that Rolls-Royces are so expensive.

3 I *am sorry* I bought these shoes.

4 *It is a pity* you persist in doing these stupid things.

5 I *am sorry* Aunt Victoria isn't coming to our party.

6 *It's a pity* you waste your time so foolishly.

7 *I'm sorry* I had to bring the plumber for such a small job. *It's a pity* I could not do it myself.

8 Clive *is sorry* that he did not take the opportunity that we offered him.

9 *It is a pity* that your mother is such an interfering woman. *I'm sorry* she won't stop meddling in our affairs.

10 I don't think I should drive, after all. *It's a pity* I had that last drink at their party.

11 Father *is sorry* he has to get up so early tomorrow.

12 Brian says he*'s sorry* he couldn't do what you asked him to.

13 If Evelyn hadn't stayed on late to finish the job, he *would have been sorry* he didn't.

14 You always forget to take your medicine at the right time. *It's a pity* you aren't more careful.

15 I*'m sorry* we can't find a taxi. It's an awful long way to walk.

16 *It's a pity* we couldn't get seats for anything last summer at the Salzburg Festival.

17 The manager later said he *was sorry* he had left before we arrived at his office.

18 I *am sorry* we didn't choose a slightly less expensive hotel to stay at.

19 We advised Bess to bring her umbrella and now she*'s sorry* that she didn't.

20 I*'m sorry* that you have to be asked to resign your membership of this club.

74 The numbered blank spaces in this passage are each followed by three words in parentheses. In some cases, all three of these words could be used to fill the blank spaces; in other cases, only two could be used; in other cases, only one. Make your choice now.

It .... 1 (appears / seems / looks) that European homes in the fifteenth century, even the most affluent, were very .... 2 (poorly / barely / scarcely) furnished. .... 3 (Barely / Scarcely / Hardly) any .... 4 (articles / items / pieces) of furniture .... 5 (appear / happen / arrive) in our richest surviving sources of documentary evidence: the hundreds of .... 6 (wills / wishes / testaments) and inventories which .... 7 (notice / remark / mention) various items as possessions .... 8 (worthy / capable / fit) of inheritance. There were, ... 9 (naturally / consequently / typically), the bare essentials, tables and benches and cupboards, but they were .... 10 (roughly / crudely / rudely) made and .... 11 (intended / meant / supposed), one guesses, to be eventually chopped .... 12 (up / down / round) for firewood, and replaced without any .... 13 (thought / idea / opinion). Ideas of comfort and luxury were concentrated on the great beds, natural enough .... 14 (when / if / unless) we remember that it was not unusual for the .... 15 (whole / entire / all) family and their guests to .... 16 (share / divide / separate) the same bed-chamber. Beds were notable mainly for their rare and costly hangings and covers, which were regarded as property of importance .... 17 (until / to / on) a comparatively late date, and .... 18 (left / discarded / bequeathed) just like gold or land. Tapestries and fabrics of the most varied description were often magnificent, imparting to the great castles a certain barbaric splendour .... 19 (heightened / swelled / increased) by gilding and the common .... 20 (practice / habit / custom) of painting the walls and woodwork of the rooms in brilliant colours.

75 Rephrase each of these sentences in such a way that you can use the word that appears in capital letters. Do not change this word in any way.

EXAMPLE Fish for breakfast doesn't appeal to everyone. TASTE
ANSWER Fish for breakfast is not to everyone's taste.

1 Have you any objection to my sitting here for a few minutes? MIND

2 I'm going to make you responsible for today's programme. CHARGE

3 The firm is going to raise everybody's salary. GIVEN

4 Did Pamela say why she was so late? REASON

5 It wasn't necessary for you to do all that washing-up. NEEDN'T

6 Things are always going wrong in a job like this. SORT

7 The agent said it is a magnificent, eighteenth-century mansion. DESCRIBED

8 We were just going to bed when the earthquake happened. POINT

9 Tony bought Stella a necklace as a compensation for not having a holiday. MAKE

10 The doctor says that Stanley's liver will be all right now, unless he starts drinking again. PROVIDED

11 The stories he tells about his war experiences are unbelievable. BEYOND

12 My car costs me an awful lot to run these days. SPEND

13 It's a month now since she fell down the stairs but you can still see the bruises. SHOW

14 The garden is too small for us to build a swimming pool. ROOM

15 What speed is allowed on this motorway? HOW

16 It is as though they were millionaires, the way they live! MIGHT

17 We could have walked to the station, it was so near. A taxi wasn't at all necessary. ENOUGH

18 There's no need to telephone me when you arrive. BOTHER

19 Is it really advisable to freeze this sort of food? SHOULD

20 Nobody would let me go into the hospital to see the survivors. ALLOWED

76 Here are twenty nouns arranged in alphabetical order. Rearrange them in five groups, bringing together those which are similar or related in meaning. Each group will have four nouns.

associate	fear	mate	partner	sarcasm
colleague	fright	mockery	path	terror
command	irony	order	regulation	track
direction	lane	panic	ridicule	way

77 As was seen in Exercise 52, there are about sixty idiomatic comparisons in English like *as mad as a hatter* (meaning *extremely* mad) and *as poor as a church mouse* (meaning *extremely* poor). Here are another twenty. Can you complete them?

1 as happy as a ....
2 as firm as a ....
3 fat as a ....
4 as easy as ....
5 as sour as ....
6 as tough as ....
7 as ugly as ....
8 as white as a ....
9 as dry as a ....
10 as red as a ....
11 as .... as a flash.
12 as .... as a new pin.
13 as .... as a judge.
14 as .... as putty.
15 as .... as a cucumber.
16 as .... as a doornail.
17 as .... as gold.
18 as .... as the driven snow.
19 as .... as a ghost.
20 as .... as pitch.

78 In the blank spaces in these sentences, put *some* or *any* or *one* or *ones*, as appropriate.

EXAMPLE May I borrow a book for the weekend? .... book will do. I just want to have .... thing to read.

ANSWER ... *Any* book will do. I just want to have *something* to read.

1 I want .... mangoes, please, if you have .... fresh .... I don't want tinned ....

2 .... stupid man has parked his car across our gate, and I can't get out! How can .... body be so thoughtless?

3 I gave the papers to every .... in the class, except of course the .... who had already come to the office to take them.

4 It's such a lovely day that we ought to make .... sandwiches and take .... nice cold beer and go off .... where in the country. I don't mind where. .... where will be better than here in the town.

5 I'm not feeling very well tonight. I'd better not have .... thing heavy for supper. Could you make me .... soup instead?

6 Good! They've given him a reward. .... one who behaves as bravely as he did certainly deserves ....

7 I seldom understand .... thing of what he says. I suppose .... people do, though .... one who does must have .... power of thought-reading!

8 We went round the meeting with a collecting box. About twenty people did not give .... thing at all, but the .... who did give .... thing were quite generous. In all, we collected .... twenty-five pounds.

9 Eric has at last bought the Mercedes station-wagon he's been saving up for. Have you seen it? It's really .... car!

10 You would think he would have been able to answer .... of these questions, wouldn't you? It wasn't as if there were .... with .... unusual difficulties.

79 Finish each of the incomplete sentences below in such a way that it has the same meaning as the sentence above it.

EXAMPLE It would be wise for us to take raincoats.
We'd ....
ANSWER We'd better take raincoats.

1. I don't like this food as much as you do.
You ....

2. What particularly impressed me was her accent-free pronunciation.
I ....

3. The result of the match was never in doubt.
At no time ....

4. This will be the orchestra's first performance outside London.
This will be the first time ....

5. How long has this roof been leaking?
When ....

6. A waiter spilled soup over Lydia's new dress last night.
Lydia ....

7. I haven't heard from home recently.
My ....

8. I suppose you didn't enjoy that party very much, did you?
You can't ....

9. It's a good thing I had my cheque-book on me. We would have been in trouble otherwise.
If ....

10. It would be a good idea if you went and asked her yourself.
You'd ....

11. The violent criticism of the Prime Minister was quite unjustified.
There ....

12. Whose is that car outside the gate?
Who does ....?

13. If it doesn't rain soon, a lot of our crops will be lost.
Unless ....

14 It won't make any difference if it rains because we'll still go.
We'll still go ....

15 I would do anything in the world for him.
There's ....

16 Veronica remembered and so did Dorothy.
Veronica didn't ....

17 What would your own reaction have been?
What reaction ....?

18 Aren't they ever going to bring us the breakfast I ordered for 8 o'clock?
Aren't we ....

19 The people who were there can remember nothing unusual happening.
Nobody who ....

20 It was my refusal to obey the policeman that caused my arrest.
It was because I ....

80 Make all the changes and additions necessary to produce, from the following ten groups of words and phrases, a complete letter from Colin in Brighton, England to Georgos in Athens, Greece. (See Exercise 7 for an example, if necessary.)

Dear Georgos,

So glad / get / letter / learn / you able / come / spend / part summer holiday / here

1 ....
....

Doubt / weather / so good / as / Greece / but hope / not / too bad

2 ....

Sea / not more / fifteen minutes / house / perhaps / bathing / possible

3 ....

At first / you / find / sea / cold / particularly / you accustomed / Mediterranean / but / soon / used to it

4 ....
....

Unfortunately / not manage / come London / meet you / but if / you able / get / train / Brighton / I / meet you / station

5 ....
....

Only hour / journey / train / London Brighton / from / Victoria Station

6 ....

It / become / easier / quicker / reach / Victoria Station

7 ....

Simply / take / airport bus / now / go / direct / Grosvenor Gardens / opposite / station

8 ....
   ....

   When / Victoria / telephone / me / tell / arrival / time / Brighton / you / already / have / number / last letter

9 ....
   ....

   When / reach / Brighton / expect you / recognise / me / photograph / but I / wearing / carrying / depending weather / light-grey raincoat / make / extra sure

10 ....
   ....
   ....

   Looking forward to seeing you,
   Yours ever,
   Colin

81 The word in *capital letters* at the end of each of these sentences can be changed in such a way that it forms a word that fits suitably in the blank space. Fill each blank in this way.

   EXAMPLE   The bloodstain on her dress was very .... NOTICE
   ANSWER   The bloodstain on her dress was very *noticeable*.

   1 Kenneth gave the child a .... of sweets. HAND

   2 The discussion was brought to a .... conclusion. SATISFY

   3 Unless you measure with the greatest ...., the door will not fit properly and we shall have trouble with it. ACCURATE

   4 So many strikes are a great .... to the country's economic recovery. HINDER

   5 No, this is not an original; it's a good ...., though. PRODUCE

6 In his .... to make himself understood, he spoke too slowly and too loudly. ANXIOUS

7 After the children had gone back to school, the house was .... quiet. COMPARE

8 Now that she has got a job, Lena is .... of her parents. DEPEND

9 It's quite .... to ask him again. He'll never agree. POINT

10 If you behave with this sort of .... to your other customers, I don't think you'll remain in business long. POLITE

11 The speaker showed his nervousness by constantly .... his tie. STRAIGHT

12 We'd better go by train. The car is too .... for such a long journey. RELY

13 Is there any difference between egoism and ....? SELF

14 It is dangerous for an .... driver to drive a car in the centre of Paris during the mid-day rush. EXPERIENCE

15 After the death of her parents, Lisa was brought up in an .... ORPHAN

16 Douglas, now that you're the head of the family, you must take your .... place at the head of the table. RIGHT

17 There is always a .... of fresh vegetables at this time of the year. SCARCE

18 Did you really have to behave with such .... to the little girl? SEVERE

19 I need a new secretary. I want someone who is charming, efficient and absolutely .... TRUST

20 In these days of terrorism and hijacking, ... at airports must be made a lot tighter. SECURE

82 In these sentences, change *any* or its compounds (*anyone*, *anything*, etc.) into *no* or its compounds (*no one*, *nothing*, etc.), or *none*. Make whatever other changes are necessary.

EXAMPLE 1   I decided not to ask him *any* more questions.
ANSWER   I decided to ask him *no* more questions.

EXAMPLE 2   We've just looked in the box for letters. There aren't *any*.
ANSWER   ……… There are *none*.

1 Oh dear, we can't have a bath. There isn't any hot water left.
2 At the party last night, we didn't see anybody we knew very well.
3 You can't find anything like this outside Austria.
4 There aren't any more eggs in the refrigerator.
5 We didn't go anywhere else that weekend.
6 They decided not to do any more work that day.
7 I would lend you the money if I could but I haven't any to spare.
8 You ask me how much chance he has of succeeding. I'm sorry to say I don't think he has any at all.
9 Oh dear! The baker has closed and we haven't any bread. We might have crispbread instead, you say? It would be a good idea – except for the fact that we haven't any of that either.
10 Let's go to bed early. There isn't anything on TV worth staying up for.

83 Fill each of the numbered blank spaces in this passage with ONE suitable word.

.... 1 had been an unusually peaceful evening, ... 2 no arguments or disagreements, and Susan and Jack were reading comfortably in their chairs. Jack did not notice when Susan .... 3 her book down. He turned a page and read several lines before she spoke.

'He was *such* a nice man,' she said, as .... 4 to herself.

Jack read as .... 5 as the middle of the page before he really .... 6 in what she had said. He looked over his book at her.

'Did you say something?', he asked, ... 7 his place in the book with his finger.

Susan .... 8 her head. 'No, dear. It wasn't anything. I didn't .... 9 to interrupt. Just go on with your reading.'

Jack .... 10 her thoughtfully for a moment, and went back to his book. He tried to go on with his reading. It was impossible.

'Who was so nice?' he demanded. 'Who was this wonderful person who was so nice?'

'What did you say, dear?' said Susan, and then, as if coming back from .... 11 away, 'Oh, that!'

'............ 12?' said Jack, putting down his book.

Susan looked at him for a moment, as though examining him. 'It was Toby Hyde. Someone I used to know when I was a girl. Before your .... 13. I was .... 14 remembering how nice he was.'

'Oh,' said Jack.

'To his wife,' said Susan. .... 15 was nothing really special in her voice. .... 16 else in the world would have heard anything special in it. But Jack .... 17. He .... 18 his memory for anything Susan had been upset about. He didn't find anything, or, at least, anything recent. 'I was just thinking about him,' Susan went on. 'He was a High Court Judge.'

'Was he?' said Jack. 'Was he indeed?'

'Once, when his wife had a cold, he closed his court for the whole day so that he could stay at home with her. Wasn't that nice?'

116

'I .... 19 if you have your facts .... 20,' said Jack. 'A High Court Judge doesn't close his court for a whole day because his wife has a cold.'

'I assure you he did,' said Susan. 'He was that sort of a nice man.'

84 Choose from the four phrases in *italics* after each of the following sentences the one which most suitably fills the blank space.

1 It has been raining steadily and continuously for three days .... now.
at an end   on end   in the end   no end

2 The prisoner ran .... down the hill and escaped.
in full swing   at full tilt   to the full   full length

3 He asked her so many times to do it that .... she did so.
at the end   in the end   to the end   by the end

4 I expect you to use your ability ...., and then write a report about what you did.
in full bloom   in full   to the full   in full swing

5 Several new hotels have been built along the coast, and they have helped the tourist business ....
at an end   no end   on end   on the end

6 My brother plays his records .... in his room at night, and nobody can get enough sleep.
at full tilt   in full swing   at full blast   in full cry

7 We're selling the hotel .... of the summer, and retiring.
on the end   at the end   in the end   to the end

8 Our guest of honour arrived rather late. The party was already ....
in full swing   at full tilt   in full bloom   to the full

9 The meeting, ladies and gentlemen, is now ....
at an end   at the end   on end   to the end

10   The poor man had fallen .... in front of a bus.
    in full   full length   in full cry   at full tilt

11   .... of the month, I hope I shall have lost another two kilos.
    At the end   In the end   To the end   By the end

12   This year the roses were .... a month earlier than usual.
    in full cry   in full swing   in full bloom   at full blast

13   I found the book rather dull. I couldn't read it ....
    by the end   to the end   on the end   at an end

14   Tell me .... what happened after Jennings hit the Minister.
    to the full   in full   full length   full time

15   Eustace was standing .... of the diving board, showing off his physique.
    on the end   by the end   to the end   in the end

85 Form questions to which these sentences could be the answers. the information which is required is shown by the words in *italics*. (Imagine that somebody has spoken and you did not hear these particular words. You are now asking what they were.)

EXAMPLE 1   *Liz* broke her leg.
ANSWER   Who broke her leg?

EXAMPLE 2   Liz broke *her leg*.
ANSWER   What did Liz break?

EXAMPLE 3   Liz *broke her leg*.
ANSWER   What did Liz do?

1   I've forgotten *Amelia's address*.
2   I've forgotten *Amelia's* address.
3   We're going to *the south of France* next month.
4   We're going to *the south* of France next month.
5   We're going to the south of France *next month*.
6   We're going to the south of France *next* month.

7 Their house was struck by *lightning* again last night.

8 Their house *was struck by lightning* again last night.

9 They say that *lightning* doesn't strike twice in the same place.

10 It's about *300 kilometres* from Salzburg to Vienna.

11 It's about *300* kilometres from Salzburg to Vienna.

12 It's about 300 kilometres from *Salzburg* to Vienna.

13 It's about 300 kilometres from Salzburg to *Vienna*.

14 The thing that Mildred wants most is *a quiet house in country*.

15 *Mildred* is the one who wants a quiet house in the country.

16 A *quiet* house in the country is the thing that Mildred wants most.

17 Conrad has to take *vitamin* tablets twice a day to build up his strength.

18 Conrad has to take vitamin tablets *twice a day* to build up his strength.

19 Conrad has to take vitamin tablets *twice* a day to build up his strength.

20 Conrad has to take vitamin tablets twice a day *to build up his strength*.

86 Fill each blank space with a phrase made from *get*.

EXAMPLE   No, he wasn't sent to prison. He .... with a fine.
ANSWER   *got off*

1. I wonder whether Denise will ever .... her shyness.
2. What time did you .... home last night?
3. We're hoping to be able to .... for the weekend.
4. I don't want to go to their party but I don't see how I can .... it.
5. How are you .... with your new neighbours?

Fill each blank space with a phrase made from *take*.

EXAMPLE   I didn't .... the new boss at first, but I've come to like him a lot.
ANSWER   *take to*

6. Oh, I'm so sorry. I .... somebody from the Electricity Company.
7. Bridget .... her mother for obstinacy and meanness.
8. I shall sue him for libel unless he .... what he said about me.
9. Granny spends too much time alone in her flat. We ought to .... much more than we have been doing.
10. The manager is retiring. I wonder who is going to .... his job?

Fill each blank space with a phrase made from *make*.

EXAMPLE I think your face is much prettier without that ....

ANSWER *make-up*

11 The man was so drunk that we could not .... what he was trying to say.

12 Duncan entered the hotel and .... the bar.

13 We're awfully late. Let's run and .... lost time.

14 Telephone the police and tell them that our plumber has .... all the silver in the house.

15 If you don't want this wooden box I could .... a nice bookcase ....

87 Here are twenty sentences each with a blank space. Below each one are four words or phrases. Choose which one of these most suitably fills the blank space.

1. My uncle was .... by a gang of terrorists last week.
   slaughtered destroyed murdered assassinated

2. The meteorologists say we're likely to have a .... winter.
   calm soft mild smooth

3. Timothy has lost a lot of money these last years in the casino. He is a .... gambler.
   impulsive compulsive compelled impelled

4. Please take your place in the ....
   queue tail row file

5. I admit I suffer from a .... of patience with such people.
   shortage lack emptiness limit

6. There was another serious .... of cholera there last month.
   breakout outbreak overflow fallout

7. I can't understand how your father managed to .... that man. He had deceived all the rest of us.
   see against see through see to see out

8. Four metres of this material .... at £24.50.
   add up fetch down work out come through

9. The idea of a balanced diet is very difficult to .... to anyone who knows nothing about food values.
   put through take in put across make over

10. You must move your car at once, Madam; .... I shall have to give you a ticket.
    therefore otherwise consequently whether

11. I'm sorry to hear that Peter and Dick have .... They were such good friends.
    fallen out fallen against dropped out dropped against

12. The .... of gold has fallen slightly in the last year.
    rate value currency exchange

13 Owing to the bad weather, the garden party was ....
called off   shouted out   spoken against   cried down

14 His house is a .... between a palace and a hotel.
combination   union   cross   link

15 I'm afraid it didn't .... my mind that they weren't the right people to invite.
pass   cross   cover   fill

16 From now on everything will be .... sailing, I hope. No more problems.
simple   straight   plain   pretty

17 Peter, you're a stupid little boy! Stop .... like that.
making up   acting out   doing up   showing off

18 There was so much noise that we could hardly .... what the speaker was saying.
take in   take up   bring in   bring out

19 There is a beautiful .... of the old city from the terrace of their mountain house.
view   aspect   vision   appearance

20 Since his wife died, Roland has gone to ....
fragments   pieces   bits   scraps

88 The vocabulary of the things we eat. Can you think of the names of:
   a Ten types of seafood (e.g. *salmon*)
   b Ten types of meat (or poultry or game) (e.g. *beef*, *chicken*)
   c Fifteen types of vegetable (e.g. *cabbage*)
   d Ten types of fruit (e.g. *banana*)

89 The blank spaces in these sentences need either *the* or *a(an)* or no article at all. Say which.

1. Hold on .... 1 moment, please. I think he's still in .... 2 bed, but he might just be in .... 3 bathroom. I'll go and have .... 4 look.

2. After .... 5 awful accident he had .... 6 last month, he spent .... 7 week in .... 8 hospital. He had .... 9 private room which had .... 10 visitor's bed in it, so his wife was able to spend .... 11 lot of .... 12 time with him at .... 13 hospital.

3. To enter the British Foreign Service, it is necessary to be .... 14 graduate of .... 15 university, with .... 16 high-grade pass, and to know .... 17 two foreign languages (although it is .... 18 good thing to know .... 19 third, if possible).

4. We don't go to .... 20 cinema as often as we used to, because .... 21 most of .... 22 films that are made these days are so poor that they are not worth .... 23 price of .... 24 ticket, never mind .... 25 trouble of getting there.

5. At .... 26 cottage which she bought in .... 27 country .... 28 last year, Nora found .... 29 snake on .... 30 floor of .... 31 bedroom. She jumped on .... 32 bed and shouted for .... 33 help. Her husband came and killed it. It was .... 34 good thing he managed to do so without .... 35 trouble because it was later found to have been of .... 36 dangerous species.

6. Our grandparents have booked themselves on .... 37 tour that leaves in .... 38 second week of .... 39 next month, and brings them back in .... 40 last week before .... 41 Easter. They are going to see .... 42 famous sights: .... 43 Louvre in .... 44 Paris, ... 45 Parthenon in .... 46 Athens, and so on. .... 47 tour starts in .... 48 Hague in .... 49 Netherlands, where they now live.

7 .... 50 clock on .... 51 dome of .... 52 Town Hall began to strike .... 53 hour of seven. Always fearful of .... 54 noise, ... 55 hundreds of .... 56 pigeons there rose in .... 57 air and fluttered over .... 58 enormous roof. .... 59 few flew away, across .... 60 market place, and came to .... 61 rest on .... 62 nearby window-sills.

8 We saw your sister being interviewed on .... 63 T.V. at .... 64 weekend. You didn't see her yourself? What .... 65 pity! It was .... 66 interesting programme. She was talking about .... 67 biography she is writing about .... 68 Prime Minister.

9 .... 69 few of us are about to go by .... 70 boat to Ouranoupolis, ... 71 port at .... 72 foot of .... 73 Mount Athos. We shall then go on and upwards by .... 74 donkey and visit some of .... 75 monasteries. Only .... 76 men in our group are going, though. .... 77 women are not allowed on .... 78 Mount Athos.

10 Eustace, as usual, was .... 79 first to arrive at .... 80 party we gave .... 81 last night, and .... 82 last to leave. And for .... 83 most of .... 84 meantime he just stood near .... 85 bar, drinking steadily.

90 Rephrase each of these sentences by replacing the word that appears in *italics* with a phrase of similar meaning *containing a noun*, and making all other necessary changes.

EXAMPLE 1   The dog was *chained* to a post outside the shop.
ANSWER   The dog was *fastened by chain* to a post outside the shop.

EXAMPLE 2   Mortimer usually *walks* to his office every morning.
ANSWER   Mortimer usually *goes* to his office every morning *on foot*.

1 We have *credited* the money to your current account at this bank.
2 Montague was busy *oiling* his shotgun.
3 The road to the farm has at last been *asphalted*.
4 They are going to *film* the story of her life.
5 My wife is very fond of *gardening*.
6 Enemy planes *bombed* the centre of the city.
7 I want to *reserve* two seats for this evening's performance.
8 Your name *heads* the list of successful applicants.
9 Cynthia spent two years *nursing* in this hospital before she got married.
10 As the police approached, the demonstrators *stoned* them.
11 Aunt Florence spent the morning *weeding* the lawn.
12 Waiter, may we *order* now, please?
13 Since my accident, I have been finding it difficult to *lace* my shoes.
14 The policeman was so unhelpful that my aunt just couldn't *control* her temper.
15 Because the date isn't quite definite yet, I have only *pencilled* it on these papers.

91 Fill the blank spaces in these sentences with either

  a an appropriate form of the verb *use*

   EXAMPLE I wish you would stop .... my toothbrush, Ernest.
   ANSWER using

or b used to

   EXAMPLE Ian .... play squash a lot, but he prefers tennis now.
   ANSWER used to

or c an appropriate form of *get used to, be used to, become used to* or *grow used to*

   EXAMPLE I know it's very noisy here, but you'll soon .... it.
   ANSWER get / be / become / grow used to

1 The children became irritable and naughty because they .... staying up so late.

2 Cindy is still too young to .... a knife and fork.

3 When I was younger I .... go skiing whenever I could.

4 Do you mind having this macaroni today instead of the brand you usually ....?

5 I .... a taxi at all since they put up their fares so high last year.

6 We've lived here so long that we .... the heat and humidity.

7 What is that room going .... for?

8 Don't buy any more butter today. We .... up all this packet yet.

9 During the war many people .... sleeping even during air raids.

10 I .... know how to do this, but I seem to have forgotten.

11 Do try to clean this pan without .... scouring powder.

12 Young Freddy has promised .... his handkerchief again to clean his shoes.

13 Since last May we .... gas instead of electricity for cooking.

14 Until six months ago, Milly .... driving only on quiet country roads but then her husband persuaded her to try .... driving in the town too.

15 Kate .... a lot of butter for cooking but she prefers oil now.

92 Certain standard pairs of words, joined by *and*, are commonly used in English:

e.g. *bits and pieces, dead and buried, facts and figures*

In the left-hand column below are the first part of fifteen other pairs, in alphabetical order. In the right-hand column are the second part of the pairs, also in alphabetical order.

a Match the pairs.

b Put each pair into a sentence that illustrates its meaning or use.

1	cock and	a	blood
2	cut and	b	bull
3	flesh and	c	chattels
4	goods and	d	cons
5	hard and	e	dried
6	head and	f	ends
7	hide and	g	fast
8	high and	h	mighty
9	odds and	i	nail
10	prim and	j	proper
11	pros and	k	seek
12	sick and	l	shoulders
13	spick and	m	span
14	tooth and	n	tear
15	wear and	o	tired

93 Rephrase each of these sentences in such a way that you can use the words in CAPITAL LETTERS at the end of each sentence. Do not alter this word in any way.

EXAMPLE Was it really necessary for you to go there? HAVE
ANSWER   Did you really have to go there?

1. Yes, I remembered to give her your message. FORGET
2. Brown's Hotel is regarded by many people as one of the best in London. CONSIDER
3. The weather was so mild that we didn't need coats. SUCH
4. Winston says that he didn't have anything to do with the matter. DENIES
5. Virginia learned to ski when she was five years old. AGE
6. I slept for only three hours last night. HAD
7. I would have telephoned you as promised if my brother had not suddenly arrived. BECAUSE
8. It's no use trying to mend this tyre. POINT
9. I'm not going to punish you this time. LET
10. Christina inherited a large fortune on her father's death. CAME
11. All of us except Timothy thought the hotel was worth its high prices. ONLY
12. His second book is nothing like so interesting as his first was. LESS
13. What's your preference for tonight? The theatre or the cinema? RATHER
14. The murderer wiped the gun in case his fingerprints should betray him. GIVE
15. It's going to be awfully expensive. COST
16. Who is responsible for all this mess? BLAME
17. Unlike you, I don't have to retire when I'm sixty. DIFFERENCE

18 It would not be a waste of time to look at that house again. WORTH

19 We see it as a wonderful opportunity. LOOK

20 There is almost nothing in the house to eat tonight. HARDLY

94 Here are fifteen common words, printed in CAPITAL LETTERS. Following each one are four other words. Two of these can combine with the 'head-word' to form common standard compounds (sometimes as a single word, sometimes with a hyphen and sometimes as two separate words).

Say which the two words are, then either make sentences using the compounds or say what they mean.

EXAMPLE GATE break – crash – route – way
ANSWER   crash, way
    1 gatecrash: to gain admission to a social gathering without an invitation.
    2 gateway: an opening in a wall, fence or hedge that is closed by a gate.

1 CROSS   answer – question – street – word
2 FRUIT   engine – fly – machine – wasp
3 GAS   eye – light – mask – room
4 GIRL   friend – hood – mate – wish
5 HIGH   meal – land – night – tea
6 MOUTH   moisture – organ – part – piece
7 OIL   cloth – coat – field – material
8 POST   case – day – mark – script
9 ROUND   about – down – route – trip
10 SUN   chair – heat – stroke – tan
11 SUNDAY   best – school – time – worst
12 TEST   case – place – room – tube
13 TOOTH   ache – doctor – pain – pick

14 WHIP   hand – mark – round – string

15 WORK   room – shop – time – wish

95 The numbered blank spaced in these sentences are each followed by three words or phrases in parentheses. In some cases all three of these words or phrases could be used to fill the blank spaces; in other cases only two could be used; in other cases, only one. Make your choice now.

It is widely .... 1 (acknowledged / admitted / adopted) among men that all babies are very ugly, and it is with feelings .... 2 (hardly / barely / scarcely) raised above the level of pity that one of them will .... 3 (watch / gaze / look) upon the newly-born .... 4 (infants / offspring / offshoots) of his friends. How strange it is, he tells himself, that poor old .... 5 (So-and-so / What's-his-name / Who-and-who) should have such a horrible child when he is such a fine-looking fellow with a quite attractive wife. What an awful sight the little creature is with its ugly nose and hungry red face, and how extraordinary that anything so small .... 6 (should / ought to / can) produce such a terrible volume of sound! He .... 7 (racks / screws / twists) his brain for something suitable to say to the parents. Nothing comes, for he .... 8 (hardly likes / scarcely loves / does not want) to display his ignorance by asking .... 9 (what sex it is / about its sex / for its sex). He .... 10 (saves / is saved / may be saved) from complete mental paralysis by the usual unimaginative reference to its resemblance to its father or mother. It is with a sigh of relief that he sees the creature carried away, ... 11 (screaming / protesting / screeching) to another part of the house. The interview is over, and until by some miracle the creature turns into an acceptable human being he .... 12 (must not / does not have to / need not) think of it again.

.... 13 (Then / There / It) comes a time when the same man's hall is blocked by a baby-carriage. He cannot get in or out without .... 14 (banging / hitting / knocking) himself on the handle of it. He is constantly being warned to .... 15 (discuss / say / speak) in a whisper or to tread on tiptoe, and the bathroom is decorated with unfamiliar laundry drying.

.... 16 (In the end / At the end / Finally) he is persuaded to hold the cause of all this trouble and, approaching it as he would approach an unexploded bomb, he wraps his arms around it .... 17 (in case / for fear / if) it should fall to pieces. He peers doubtfully at the face of his baby. .... 18 (To / With / In) his surprise he sees no ugly nose, no hungry red face, no dribbling mouth. Instead he sees the pleasant face, the classic profile, the gentle smile of recognition.

It is only .... 19 (an affair / a matter / a question) of time before he, in his turn, will be proudly producing photographs from his wallet, and failing .... 20 (altogether / entirely / completely) to notice the look of boredom on the faces of his friends.

96 One of the seven adverb particles shown below can be used *before* each of the verbs in these sentences for the formation of a noun. Can you say which one is needed?

by   down   in   on   out   over   up

EXAMPLE   With the new machines the .... put of the factory has increased enormously.

ANSWER   *out*put

1 The .... keep of a car as large as yours must cost an awful lot these days.

2 There's no need to drive through that city now, thank goodness. They've built a .... pass.

3 What was the .... come of the meeting? Did you reach a decision?

4 The .... set of breast cancer is usually shown by a lump under the skin.

5 During the broadcasting of a radio programme, there is often a lot of amusing .... play.

6 Arnold's daily .... take of alcohol must give his liver a lot too much work.

7 We had hoped that rain would stay away during our garden party but a sudden .... pour sent everybody scurrying inside the house.

8 The communists have been plotting the .... throw of this government for years now, but they haven't much hope.

9 Poor Hugh killed himself with an .... dose of barbiturates.

10 Football is a useful .... let for people's feelings of anger and frustration.

11 I don't understand how that man manages to run two cars on a junior clerk's .... come.

12 Inefficiency and overspending were basically the cause of the .... fall of the previous government.

13 I wonder what was really the reason for Father's .... burst of anger at breakfast?

14 Judith was in bed over the weekend with a serious stomach .... set.

15 Roger understood what was in my mind almost before I started to speak. He's very quick on the .... take.

97 Read through this passage and then look at the exercise that follows it.

Mr Phanourakis was eighty-five years old when he said goodbye to his Greek mountain village and took an American ship for the United States. His sons had done well in the restaurant business there and wanted him to spend his remaining years with them.

The old gentleman knew no language save his own but, with the dignified self-confidence of the Greek mountain villager, he made his way easily about the foreign ship. When the bell announced the serving of lunch on his first day on board he found the number of his table on the passenger-list outside the dining room and went straight to it while most of the others waited for the chief steward to tell them where to sit.

It was a small table for two. Mr Phanourakis sat down. After a few moments his table companion arrived. 'Bon appétit, m'sieur,' he murmured politely, as he took the other chair.

Mr Phanourakis looked at him quickly, and then smiled. 'Phanourakis,' he said, carefully spacing out the Greek syllables.

During the afternoon one of the ship's officers, who spoke some Greek, asked the old gentleman if he had found any acquaintances on board.

Mr Phanourakis shook his head. 'No,' he said, 'the only person I've met so far is my table companion. He must be French. His name is Bonapetit – or something like that.'

'That is not his name,' said the officer gently. 'It is a French expression that means "Good appetite".'

'Oh,' said the old gentleman quietly. 'It was very foolish of me to misunderstand.'

At dinner time he found the Frenchman already at the table. He smiled shyly, sat down, and said carefully, 'Bon appétit, m'sieur.'

The Frenchman returned his smile. 'Phanourakis, m'sieur,' he said.

Here are some sentences from the passage with a number of words or phrases in *italics*. Rephrase each of the sentences in such a way that you keep the original meaning but *do not use any word or phrase that is printed in italics*. You may freely take away other words that are not in *italics*, but you must make sure that the sentence remains grammatically correct.

In some cases a simple synonym may be all that is needed:

EXAMPLE   Ingrid drank no beverage *apart from* tea.
ANSWER   Ingrid drank no beverage *but* tea.

In other cases a change of construction and the use of different words may be needed:

EXAMPLE   They wanted him to spend his *remaining years* with them.
ANSWER   They wanted him to spend *the rest of his life* with them.

1 Mr Phanourakis was eighty-five years *old* when he *said goodbye to* his Greek mountain village.

2 His sons had *done well* in the restaurant business there.

3 The old gentleman knew *no* language *save his own*.

4 He *made* his way *easily* about the foreign ship.

5 *Most* of the others waited for the chief steward to tell them *where to sit*.

6 *After* a few moments his table companion arrived and *took* the other chair.

7 One of the ship's officers, who *spoke* some Greek, asked the old gentleman if he had found any *acquaintances* on *board*.

8 'He *must be* French. His name is Bonapetit – or something *like that*.'

9 '*It* was foolish of me to *mis*understand.'

10 The Frenchman *returned* his smile.

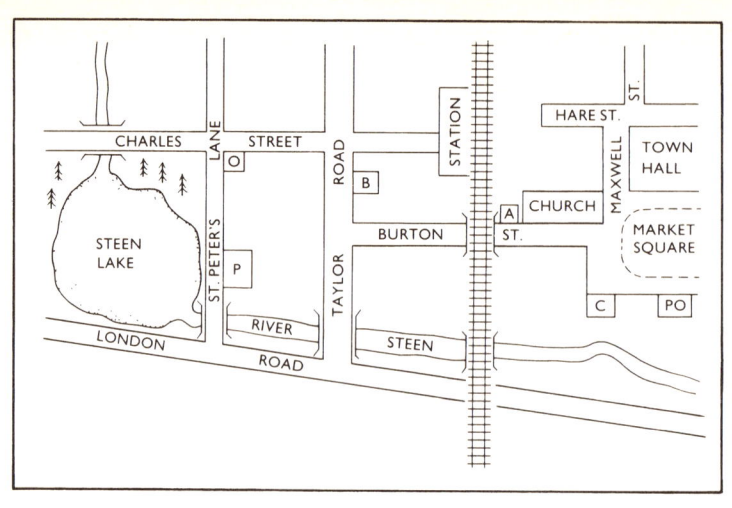

98 This map shows part of a town. Study it for a few minutes and then answer the questions below it.

1. Why can't Mr Adams, who lives at the house marked A, see the clock which is on the front of the Town Hall?
2. Why could it be pleasant to stay at the Princess Hotel (marked P)?
3. If you are in Burton Street, how do you get from one side of the railway to the other?
4. Imagine you are a policeman on duty at the railway station. Tell a visitor who has just arrived the way to the Princess Hotel.
5. Where is the Post Office (marked PO)?
6. Imagine you are staying at the Central Hotel (marked C). Which way would you go to get to Mr Brent's house (marked B)?
7. Where is the Ooh-la-la Discotheque (marked O)?
8. If you arrived in the town by train and wanted to go to Hare Street, you might feel a little annoyed. Why?
9. Why do you think the road beside the river has that particular name?
10. If you hire a canoe or rowing-boat from the garden behind the Central Hotel (marked C), where could you go in it.

99 The blank spaces in these sentences can be filled with one of the following eight words:

rarely scarcely yet never still already even frequently

1 We .... ever see him these days.
2 I eat biscuits so .... that a packet lasts me a long time.
3 I cannot .... remember what the book was about, let alone the title.
4 I .... do not know where I am going for my holidays this year.
5 We cannot tell you .... what the programme will be. Ask us again tomorrow.
6 Clara is .... having trouble with the car she bought last week.
7 Put it in the drawer. You .... know when a piece of string like that will come in useful.
8 .... had Collette got into the bath when the earthquake happened.
9 How .... do you go to the dentist for a check-up?
10 I .... wouldn't give it to you .... if you begged me on your knees.
11 We don't want to go to their party, I know, and .... I think we'll have to.
12 You've finished the job ....? My goodness, you're a fast worker!
13 Edwin .... hasn't returned those books he borrowed from us.
14 It's the second time this machine has gone wrong. It's .... the most successful thing we have bought.
15 It's after midnight and I don't think there's any chance of their arriving tonight. .... so, I think we'd better wait up for just another half-hour.

100 This passage has been divided, for your convenience, into two sections. Read each section carefully twice and then answer the questions.

Section 1
In a hot railway carriage there are two small girls and a small boy in the care of their aunt, and a bachelor who is sitting as far away from them as possible. The children are bored with the journey, and are consequently troublesome. Most of the aunt's remarks begin with 'Don't', and nearly all of the children's remarks begin with 'Why?'. The aunt tries to interest them by telling a story about a little girl who was good, and made friends with everyone on account of her goodness, and was finally saved from a mad bull by a number of rescuers who admired her goodness.

'Wouldn't they have saved her if she hadn't been good?' asked the bigger of the small girls. It was exactly the question that the bachelor had wanted to ask.
'Well, yes,' admitted the aunt weakly, 'but I don't think they
5 would have run so fast to her help if they hadn't liked her so much.'
'It's the stupidest story I've ever heard,' said the bigger of the small girls.
'I didn't listen after the first bit, it was so stupid,' said Cyril,
10 the small boy.
'You don't seem to be much of a success as a story-teller,' said the bachelor suddenly from his corner.
The aunt was annoyed at this unexpected attack. 'It's a very difficult thing to tell stories that children can both understand
15 and appreciate,' she said stiffly.
'I don't agree with you,' said the bachelor.
'Perhaps *you* would like to tell them a story,' said the aunt.
'Tell us a story,' demanded the bigger of the small girls.
'Once upon a time,' began the bachelor, 'there was a little girl
20 called Bertha, who was extraordinarily good.'
The children lost their interest at once. All stories were dreadfully alike, no matter who told them.
'She did all that she was told,' went on the bachelor, fixing his eyes on the children's, 'she was always truthful, she kept
25 her clothes clean, she ate whatever was put in front of her, learned her lessons perfectly, and was polite in her manners.'

138

'Was she pretty at least?' asked the bigger of the small girls.

'Not as pretty as either of you,' said the bachelor, 'but she was horribly good.'

30 The children's interest came back. The word 'horrible' in connection with goodness was something new to them, and they liked it.

'She was so good,' continued the bachelor, 'that she won several medals for goodness, which she always wore, pinned to 35 her dress. There was a medal for obedience, another for punctuality, and a third for good behaviour. They were large metal medals and they clinked quite loudly against one another as she walked. No other child in the town where she lived had as many as three medals, so everyone knew she must be an extra 40 good child.'

'Horribly good,' said Cyril.

'Everybody talked about her goodness, and the Prince of the country heard about it, and he said that as she was so very good she might be allowed once a week to walk in his park, which 45 was just outside the town. It was a beautiful park, and no children were ever allowed in it, so it was a great honour for Bertha to be allowed to go there.'

'Were there any sheep in the park?' demanded Cyril.

'No,' said the bachelor, 'there were no sheep.'

50 'Why weren't there any sheep?' demanded the bigger of the small girls.

The aunt permitted herself a smile of satisfaction.

'There were no sheep in the park,' said the bachelor, with no trace of hesitation, 'because the Prince's mother had once had 55 a dream that her son would be killed either by a sheep or else by a clock falling on him. For that reason the Prince never kept a sheep in his park or a clock in his palace.'

The aunt gave a small gasp of admiration.

'Was the Prince killed by a sheep or a clock?' asked Cyril.

60 'He is still alive, so we can't tell whether the dream will come true,' said the bachelor calmly. 'Anyway, there were no sheep in the park, but there were lots of little pigs running all over the place.'

'Were they dirty?' asked the smaller of the small girls.

65 'Yes, they were very dirty,' said the bachelor.

'Horribly dirty,' said Cyril, with satisfaction.

The aunt gave a sound that was like a grunt.

'Bertha was rather sorry to find that there were no flowers in

the park,' the bachelor went on. 'She had promised her aunts,
70 with tears in her eyes, that she would not pick any of the kind
Prince's flowers, and she had meant to keep her promise.'

'Why weren't there any flowers?'

'Because the pigs had eaten them all,' said the bachelor
promptly. 'The gardeners had told the Prince that you couldn't
75 have both pigs and flowers, so he had decided to have pigs and
no flowers.'

There was a murmur of approval at the excellence of the
Prince's decision.

1 Why do you think the aunt answered *weakly* (line 4)?

2 What could be a reason for the bachelor's fixing his eyes on the children's (line 23)?

3 What do you think was in the bigger girl's mind when she used the words *at least* in her question 'Was she pretty at least?' (line 27)?

4 Why did the children like the use of the word *horrible* in connection with goodness (line 30)?

5 Why did the aunt smile with satisfaction (line 52)?

6 What do the words *with no trace of hesitation* (lines 53–54) tell us about the bachelor? And which two single words, later in this section, tell us the same thing?

7 Why did the aunt gasp with admiration (line 58)?

8 Why did she later grunt (line 67)?

9 Bertha had promised that she would not pick any of the Prince's flowers. Why, then, do you think she was sorry to find there weren't any flowers in the park?

10 Rephrase the sentence *It's the stupidest story I've ever heard* (line 7) in such a way that you use the subject *I* instead of *It*.

11 Why is the indefinite article *a* used in the phrase *and a third for good behaviour* (line 36) instead of the definite article *the*?

12 Rephrase the sentence *For that reason the Prince never kept a sheep in his park or a clock in his palace* (lines 56–57) in the passive voice.

13 Rephrase the question *Was the Prince killed by a sheep or a clock?* (line 59) in the active voice.

14 Give either a word or a short phrase which could be substituted for each of these without loss of meaning:

annoyed at (line 13)   quite (line 37)   trace (line 54)
whatever (line 25)   extra (line 39)   meant (line 71)

Section 2

'There were lots of other delightful things in the park, though,' said the bachelor, 'and Bertha walked here and there, and enjoyed herself very much, and thought to herself: "If I were not so extraordinarily good, I should not have been allowed to come into this beautiful park and enjoy all that there is to be seen in it," and her three medals clinked against one another as she walked and helped to remind her how very good she really was. At that moment, a large wolf came into the park to see if it could catch a fat little pig for its supper.'

There was an immediate awakening of interest among the children.

'How large was it?' asked the bigger of the girls.

'It was enormous.'

'Did it see Bertha?' asked Cyril.

'Yes, the first thing it saw in the park was Bertha. Her dress was so spotlessly white and clean that it could be seen from a long way off. When Bertha saw that the wolf was coming towards her, she began to wish she had never been allowed to come into the park. She ran as fast as she could, and the wolf ran after her, its black tongue dripping saliva and its eyes gleaming with unspeakable ferocity. Bertha managed to reach some bushes with a strong sweet smell, and she hid herself among the branches of one of the thickest. The wolf came sniffing among the branches. Bertha was terribly frightened and thought to herself: "If I had not been so extraordinarily good, I should be safe in the town at this moment." However, the smell of the bush was so strong that the wolf could not sniff out where Bertha was hiding, so he thought he might as well go off and catch a little pig instead. But Bertha did not know this, and she was trembling with so much fear that the medal for obedience began to clink against the medals for good conduct and punctuality. The wolf was just about to move away when he heard the sound of the medals clinking and he stopped to

141

listen. They clinked again. He ran into the bush, his eyes gleaming with triumph, and he dragged Bertha out and ate her. In the end, all that was left of her were her shoes, some bits of
115 clothing, and the three medals for goodness.'
There was a pause.
The children looked at the bachelor with wide, shining eyes.
'Were any of the little pigs killed?' asked the bigger girl.
'No, they all escaped.'
120 There was another pause.
'The story began badly,' said the smaller of the girls, 'but it had a very beautiful ending.'
'It's the most beautiful story I've ever heard,' said the bigger of the girls.
125 'It's the *only* beautiful story I've ever heard,' said Cyril.
The aunt began to splutter. 'It was a most improper story to tell to young children! How did you dare! You have destroyed the effect of years of careful teaching.'
The train began to slow down.
130 'At any rate,' said the bachelor, standing up and collecting his things, 'I kept them quiet for ten minutes, which was more than you were able to do.'
'Please don't go,' said Cyril. 'Tell us another story.'

15 Why was there an awakening of interest when the wolf came into the story (line 88)?

16 Why did one of the girls ask how large it was, and why did the bachelor say it was enormous? (lines 90–91)

17 Do you think Cyril was feeling worried about Bertha when he asked if the wolf saw her (line 92)?

18 Why was there the first pause (line 116)?

19 Why did the children have wide, shining eyes (line 117)?

20 Why was there a second pause (line 120)?

21 Why was the aunt angry with the bachelor? How had he destroyed the effect of years of careful teaching?

22 On two occasions the bachelor was rather rude to the aunt. Can you say what he said on these two occasions (the first was in Section 1)? And can you think of a reason why he was rude to her?

23 Rewrite the passage from line 118 to the end, putting all the dialogue into *reported speech*. Begin: *The bigger girl asked whether*...

24 Explain in your own words the meaning of:

    a sniff out (line 105)
    b he might as well go off (line 106)
    c was just about to move away (line 110)
    d The aunt began to splutter (line 126)

25 Give either a word or short phrase which could be substituted for each of these without loss of meaning:

awakening (line 88)   gleaming (line 99)
spotlessly (line 94)   ferocity (line 99)

KEY TO THE 100 EXERCISES

KEY TO THE EXERCISES

1 (*Suggestions only. Numerous variations are possible.*)

1. Levis? There's nobody here called Levis. The name is Lewis. And I am Mrs Lewis.
2. He's ill in bed.
3. What do you mean, getting up? I told you he's ill.
4. Do you know my husband?
5. How do you know it would be a pleasure?
6. What do you want anyway?
7. Who gave you my number?
8. Then where did you get it from?
9. Why do you do that?
10. What's that?
11. I know what the *Daily Echo* is. I mean the circulation department.
12. That doesn't concern me.
13. Five o'clock! I don't get up at five o'clock.
14. I haven't got a letter-box.
15. It might be stolen.
16. Anyway, why should I want your newspaper?
17. I get that perfectly well from TV.
18. I'm not interested in more details.
19. Name some.
20. I don't go to the cinema.

2
1 said 2 tell 3 ask 4 talk 5 speak 6 ordered 7 say – tell 8 asked 9 say 10 telling 11 speak 12 order 13 talking – say 14 ask 15 talking

3
1 cheque (an IOU)
2 prescription
3 certificate
4 statement
5 manuscript / typescript
6 map / plan sketch
7 recipe
8 receipt
9 chart
10 titles /

4
1 protest 2 acceptance 3 refusal 4 suggestion 5 denial 6 invitation 7 accusation 8 complaint 9 admission 10 offer

5 (*Suggestions only*)

1 This suitcase is not big / large enough for all my things.
2 It is such a long way to their house that we can't walk there.
3 He asked us if we could guess who had just left.
4 The architect spent six months working on the plans.
5 The day she agreed to marry him was the happiest he had ever had in his life.
6 It's a long time since I saw / have seen so much rain.
7 Instead of buying a car, Malcolm bought a motor-cycle.
8 Please tell me what this letter means.
9 Unless you're wearing a jacket and tie, you can't go into that restaurant.
10 It's time we went home.
11 Sitting at a desk is the only way I can study properly.
12 Jennifer wished she had not behaved so foolishly.
13 We needn't have taken so many clothes on holiday last summer.
14 Do I really have to arrive so early?
15 The boss has had his car stolen / The boss has been robbed of his car.
16 Take an umbrella in case it rains this afternoon.
17 We spent the whole weekend working on the garden.
18 He is having two new suits made.
19 If Leonard hadn't been eating polluted shellfish, he wouldn't have felt sick.
20 I remembered to put everything in the picnic basket except the bottle opener.

6
1. industrial
2. description
3. suspicion
4. assistant
5. unemployed
6. proof
7. understanding
8. reception
9. unfriendly
10. boyhood
11. invaluable
12. possessiveness
13. unhelpful
14. shortage
15. unfortunately
16. plentiful
17. disappearance
18. decision
19. admittance
20. lengthen

7 (*Suggestions only*)

1. Thank you very much indeed for the present that has just arrived.
2. What a lovely dress! It suits me wonderfully. I am most grateful.
3. Jack and I are going to Covent Garden to celebrate this evening.
4. Placido Domingo is singing *Don Giovanni* and von Karajan is conducting.
5. Afterwards we shall go to our favourite restaurant and have champagne as it is a special occasion.
6. The twenty-first birthday is a great day in one's life, and it comes only once.
7. My next great day will be my wedding, which will probably be in spring.
8. In spite of your living so far away we both hope very much that you will come.
9. It will be easy for you to stay with us. There is plenty of space because it is such a big house.
10. I'll tell you the definite date as soon as it's fixed.

8
1. falling
2. struck / showed / chimed / sounded
3. along / up / down
4. about / around / round / over
5. pushed / thrust
6. few
7. front
8. studied / regarded
9. without
10. at
11. being
12. down
13. again
14. companion / colleague
15. corner
16. bend
17. disappear / vanish / go
18. like
19. time
20. goes

149

9 2 Omission would mean she has given somebody else till Christmas for the work to be finished.
5 Omission would mean that Van and Eva helped other people to prepare the meal.
8 Omission would mean that the wolves approached us, snarling ferociously.
10 Omission would mean that the girls happily showed other people their new dresses.

10 1 in 2 ask 3 have 4 always 5 *un*comfortable 6 *go*ing 7 *clean*ing 8 few 9 chain 10 hearts 11 cost 12 you 13 morning 14 got 15 us 16 did 17 hat 18 the 19 else 20 bath

11 1 disturb 2 wasted 3 model 4 gone up 5 limit 6 justify 7 ashamed 8 settle down 9 occur 10 mind 11 interfere 12 beat 13 solution 14 gave up 15 managed 16 fail 17 intend 18 outcome 19 existence 20 streak

12 1 hand to hand 2 in hand 3 had a hand 4 at hand 5 underhand 6 second hand 7 out of hand 8 by hand 9 on all hands 10 lend a hand

13 1 peace – piece 2 place – plaice 3 pause – paws 4 raise – rays 5 saw – sore 6 sees – seize 7 shoot – chute 8 stairs – stares 9 too – two 10 way – weigh

14
1. Parcels used to be delivered (by our postal service). Now they have to be collected (by us).
2. The production figures are said (by the company) to have fallen short of expectations.
3. Everyone has been given two weeks / Two weeks have been given to everyone (by the police) to surrender any guns which may be possessed illegally.
4. UFOs are believed by many people to exist, never mind what is said by the authorities.
5. The hospital is to be visited by the Prime Minister tomorrow.
6. This painting is believed by my family to be worth a lot of money.
7. Weren't you told that people cannot be allowed into the area unless a certificate of inoculation is produced?
8. The riot was found (by the inquiry) to have been started by anarchists.
9. Will his leg have to be amputated or will it be saved?
10. A volcano was said (by the radio) last night to be erupting on the island of Xand.
11. The factory is going to be isolated (by the authorities) because of the atomic leak.
12. He is said to have been cleaning his pistol – and his death was caused by carelessness.
13. That matter needs to be gone into (by us) very carefully.
14. The survivors of the crash are reported to be on their way to hospital.
15. In my absence the lock of my car had been broken and the luggage on the back seat (had been) stolen.
16. ... I hate being said goodbye to through the window of a train.
17. This broken glass will have to be picked up, or the children mustn't be allowed to come anywhere near this room.
18. Jackson is shown by evidence to have been inside the house at the time of the murder.
19. Am I really going to be allowed to drive your lovely Rolls-Royce?
20. The Princess is said to be staying incognito at the Hilton.

15
1. furniture
2. transport
3. meals
4. tools
5. armed forces / services
6. cruise
7. flight
8. voyage
9. travel
10. trip
11. corkscrew
12. screwdriver
13. spade
14. kettle
15. generator / dynamo

16 (*Suggestions only*)
1. she took her
2. woke him up again
3. would have sent you again
4. Unless
5. has made it
6. or I'll
7. looking forward
8. me a ring / call
9. couldn't / can't have been her
10. rather than be driven / to being driven
11. shouldn't / oughtn't to keep them
12. has been raining / has been wet
13. What's on your / Is there anything on your
14. to have gone to / to have been at
15. there were any
16. have found what is wrong with
17. turn / switch off / out
18. to have it (dry) cleaned
19. would have missed / wouldn't have caught
20. Let me / I want to

17
1. C
2. B
3. C
4. D
5. D
6. C
7. D
8. C
9. C
10. D
11. B
12. B
13. B
14. A
15. C
16. D
17. B
18. A
19. A
20. B

18
1. a Something has been stolen from the car, but we still have the car.
   b The car itself has been stolen; we no longer have it.
2. a She couldn't manage to push it.
   b She couldn't manage to start it, although she was able to push it.
3. a All the climbers had the wonderful view.
   b Only the climbers who reached the top had the wonderful view.
4. a You must pay / ask / tell somebody to polish your shoes.
   b It looks as if you have polished your shoes (yourself).
5. a Maureen wondered about her own new mackintosh.
   b Maureen wondered about the speaker's new mackintosh.
6. a They will arrive a little earlier than necessary.
   b They will arrive punctually, at the moment itself.
7. a He did other things, and making his will was the last one.
   b Making his will is something the old man would refuse to do.
8. a We *can* bathe today, if we want to.
   b We *must* bathe today – it's so warm.
9. a There's no doubt that she is a princess.
   b She's a princess. So what? Why should I be interested?
10. a ... in order to discover whether they had left or not.
    b ... and found, to our disappointment, that they were not there.
11. a This news that Adrian has brought is a bit worrying.
    b This news about Adrian is a bit worrying.
12. a All the lemon trees produced good fruit.
    b Only the trees that were given the fertiliser produced good fruit.
13. a Two people voted against our proposal.
    b Four people voted against it.
14. a He is not really a Head of State, but they treated him as though he were.
    b He is a Head of State, and they treated him accordingly.
15. a Vanessa is sorry now that she didn't (or couldn't) come to your party.
    b Vanessa was sorry at the time of the party that she couldn't come to it.

19
1 in 6 out 11 down 16 of
2 up 7 off 12 in 17 off
3 out 8 for 13 up 18 out
4 off 9 for 14 off 19 in
5 up 10 down 15 off 20 up

20 1c 2b 3g 4h 5d 6f 7a 8e

21
1 Cristoforo.
2 South. The reason: 'arrived from long since Africa and even gone north' (line 18)
3 a drowned (line 13)
  b frowned (line 22)
  c another (line 23)
4 i He had realised that there were no birds.
   ii He knew they were not late; they should already have arrived.
   iii He knew that the heat would bring them, not send them away.
5 He wanted to speak to Hannay.
6 Because the things he had seen were so strange he was probably afraid of not being believed, or of not being taken seriously.
7 i It was hot enough to bubble
   ii great swells rose from the bed of the sea (line 56)
8 Line 13: it is the possessive, i.e. Mamma Meucci's house. Line 31: it shows the omission of *ha* from *has*, i.e. Alfredo Meucci has seen …
9 i rushing wind (line 58) – no wind (line 59)
   ii oppressive air (line 59) – clear sunshine (line 60)
   iii freak storm (line 62) – clear sky (line 63).
10 The eruption of the volcano.
11 All the strange things were happening together (line 84).
12 Occasionally – once now and then (line 83).
13 i … he said wonderingly (line 15)
    ii Patch frowned, his mellow mood gone in an instant (line 22)
    iii 'Cristoforo,' he said seriously (line 29)
    iv … stirring at the back of his mind was a distinct uneasiness (line 42)

v ... this intangible thing was beginning to be creepy (line 70)
vi The things that were worrying Hannay were beginning to take root in his own mind (line 79)

14 a Aerobatics is the art of doing tricks in an aircraft, such as rolling over sideways or flying in loops. Swallows often seem to be doing the same thing.
   b The question shocked everybody.
15 a he realised   d anxiety / worry   g frightening
   b unaccountable   e close / stifling   h open-mouthed
   c omen / prediction   f unnatural

*The University of London School Examinations Board accepts no responsibility whatsoever for the accuracy or method or working in the answers given.

22

	1	1 to / past (*American English also has* of / after)	
		2 among	7 of
		3 of	8 in
41		4 out	9 about/around
42		5 of	10 in
43		6 by	11 of
49			
50	2	1 out/off	7 of
51		2 in	8 up
52		3 outside	9 with
53		4 off	10 to
54		5 before/after	11 down
55		6 with	12 in
			13 in
63			
64	3	1 through	8 to/into
65		2 down/on	9 over/across
66		3 on/to	10 to
67		4 up	11 down
68		5 for	12 on/in
69		6 in	13 like
70		7 down/away	14 on/upon
78			
79	4	1 to	14 into
80		2 up	15 to
81		3 with	16 At
82		4 up	17 at/on
83		5 to	18 with
84		6 On	19 at
85		7 for	20 like
86		8 up	21 in/at
87		9 to	22 out
88		10 for	23 in
89		11 of	24 of
90		12 until/till	25 in
91		13 up	26 of
104			
106	5	1 with	4 of/during
107		2 out	5 out/on
108		3 of	6 over/through
112			

6 1 round/around/about
   2 in
   3 near
   4 of
   5 of
   6 up
   7 of
   8 of/from
   9 of/from
   10 of
   11 of
   12 up
   13 by/in
   14 of
   15 in
   16 through
   17 in
   18 out
   19 in
   20 in/at
   21 Over/Above/In
   22 of
   23 of
   24 of

7 1 at/in
   2 in/of
   3 from
   4 to
   5 after
   6 up
   7 for
   8 at/by/near
   9 up
   10 in
   11 on
   12 of
   13 of
   14 on
   15 of

8 1 through/towards
   2 out
   3 by
   4 with/from
   5 off
   6 along
   7 like
   8 against/on
   9 off
   10 from/for
   11 over/across
   12 on

9 1 on/along
   2 out
   3 from
   4 in
   5 out
   6 at
   7 of
   8 up
   9 to
   10 into
   11 on/upon/over
   12 with
   13 off
   14 down/up/along/across
   15 with
   16 to/on/upon/round/around
   17 of

157

10 1 With
    2 in/inside
    3 like
    4 in
    5 along/up/down
    6 up/down
    7 to
    8 of
    9 from
    10 over
    11 with
    12 from
    13 to
    14 on
    15 by/past/along

23 1 The policeman told us he was sorry about it, but he would have to give us a ticket. We must surely have known that parking is / was absolutely forbidden anywhere in this / that street.
    2 Aunt Bertha said she felt rather faint. She didn't think she could go on. She told us to go on without her, all of us. She would just sit there until we came back. She would be perfectly all right.
    3 The taxi driver asked the other driver angrily why he didn't go and push a baby-carriage. He was not fit to drive a car.
    4 I heard the nurse tell him to lie still. He would pull his stitches open if he kept moving about like that.
    5 Jason told his wife that if she really did want to wear that awful skirt, he supposed he couldn't stop her. But it made her look like a sack of potatoes.
    6 The judge asked the man in the dock whether he had asked for, or received, permission to use a company car that night.
    7 Harry told his wife that he was going to see his mother that evening if he could get away from the office a little earlier. He asked her if she had any messages for his mother.
    8 Charles said that if I / she (etc.) really thought he had said that about me / her, he was not surprised that I / she was angry with him. But he assured me / her that he had not.
    9 Rosemary exclaimed that Stephen had / has some very old-fashioned ideas. They / We were / are not living in the eighteenth century. He talked / talks as though women should be seen and not heard. She had to say she was / is glad he was / is not *her* husband.
    10 Timothy asked the pretty girl at the station to let him help her with that / her suitcase. It looked a lot too heavy for her.
    11 The electrician told his assistant to hold those wires carefully. They didn't want to get a shock with *that* voltage!

12 My father said we'd better bring / take some warmer clothes with us next time we come / go here / there. It gets a lot colder in winter than he had realised.
13 My wife told me, with amusement in her eyes, that there was no sense in my getting all worn out chasing a bat with a fly-swatter. They were / are much quicker than I was / am.
14 Polly told Walter he would really have to have his hair cut soon. He was beginning to look uncouth.
15 Marilyn said she was terribly sorry she was so late. She wished she could learn to look at the clock. She asked me / us (etc.) to forgive her.
16 Gazing at the Rolls-Royce outside the hotel, Victor exclaimed at its beauty / exclaimed that it was a beauty.
17 Phyllis asked her husband severely what he had been cutting with her scissors.
18 Sylvia told the gypsy, who had his foot in the door, to go away. Otherwise she would scream – and the next-door neighbour would come running.
19 Basil said, with dignity, that as it happened he had gone there to do me / her / him a favour, not to ask for one.
20 The police inspector asked the man / him (etc.) why he was wearing that medal. He had no right to it. He had never been in any of the services.

24
1 If / Whenever
2 develops / grows
3 see / watch
4 need
5 development / progress
6 less
7 conventions / formalities
8 community / communal
9 comes
10 appreciate / value
11 maintained / said / claimed
12 based / standing
13 selfishness
14 merely / purely / simply
15 ensuring
16 view
17 individuals / people
18 full
19 talents / gifts
20 potentialities / capabilities

25 (*Suggestions only*)

1. We insist on having your answer tonight at the latest.
2. My father is going to let me borrow his car tonight.
3. We've decided to substitute these rubber shower curtains for those plastic ones
4. Somebody has robbed Miranda of all her jewellery.
5. You surely don't want a fifth icecream, do you?
6. This block of flats now belongs to the bank.
7. He was speaking too quickly for me to understand him.
8. There is absolutely nothing left in the fridge.
9. He was paying no / He wasn't paying attention to what we were saying.
10. He is afraid of nothing.
11. I am not used to getting up quite so early as this.
12. Can you direct me to the Central Post Office?
13. Nothing went wrong that morning.
14. What did you do that for?
15. Nanette never stops talking about her illnesses.
16. If I hadn't found a taxi quickly, I wouldn't have been able to catch the train.
17. The café charges a lot for a portion of strawberries and cream.
18. What chance have I of passing the examination, do you think?
19. Humphrey doesn't like cocktail parties. There's no point in asking him.
20. Please get rid of all these things.

26

1. Howard was suspicious enough of his wife to open the letter that was addressed to her.
2. The balcony was too badly built to be safe for people to stand on.
3. This hotel is too expensive for us to stay at for very long.
4. Erica is too careful to have done anything as bad as that.
5. Your feet are small enough, Madam, for you to wear the smallest of our sizes.
6. Barry was strong enough to lift the trunk on to the top of the car alone.
7. Hazel's new American car is too wide to go into her garage easily.
8. Ray is free enough this evening to help you.

9 The sky was too cloudy for us to see the UFO at all.
10 It was too late for anything to be done.
11 This little hotel is quiet and peaceful enough for us to have a really relaxing holiday.
12 Jessica is cruel enough to have been a pupil of Messalina.
13 Let's go to another beach. There are too many jelly-fish here for us to bathe in peace.
14 Please write this again, Felix. It is written too badly for me to make sense of it.
15 Richard is tall enough to change light bulbs in some rooms without having to stand on a chair.
16 It was too late when we arrived at the hotel for any food to be cooked for us.
17 Vera knows her husband's habits and movements well enough to say where he is and what he is doing at any moment.
18 This restaurant has become too expensive for many people to use.
19 The carpet was too dirty for us to clean.
20 Mother says she's getting rather too elderly to wear a bikini any longer.

27 1 g   5 t   9 a   13 h   17 f
    2 n   6 i   10 s   14 d   18 m
    3 l   7 o   11 c   15 j   19 q
    4 b   8 k   12 p   16 r   20 e

28 (*Suggestions only*)

1. The sun was shining quite brightly when Mrs Grant left home.
2. She did not think it was necessary to take an umbrella with her.
3. Soon it started raining.
4. It was still raining when the bus arrived at the market-place.
5. Mrs Grant absentmindedly took the umbrella that was hanging on the seat before her.
6. Mrs Grant went red / reddened with embarrassment and said she was sorry.
7. She tried to take no notice of the unpleasant look ...
8. Mrs Grant went directly / immediately to a shop which would sell her an umbrella.
9. She found a very pretty one and, because it was such a pretty one, decided to buy one more as a present for her daughter.
10. She did the remainder of her shopping and lunched in a café.

29

1. Anno Domini (In the year of our Lord; i.e. after Christ)
2. Before Christ
3. Central Intelligence Agency
4. Criminal Investigation Department
5. Master of Arts
6. Member of Parliament *or* Military Police
7. North Atlantic Treaty Organisation
8. Postscript (at the end of a letter)
9. Please turn over (a page)
10. Répondez, s'il vous plaît (English: Reply please)
11. Save our souls! (Distress call at sea)
12. United Kingdom (of Great Britain and Northern Ireland)
13. United Nations Educational, Scientific and Cultural Organisation
14. United Nations Organisation
15. Young Men's Christian Association

30 (*Suggestions only*)

1. He is said to have escaped to a neutral country.
2. The sand of the beach was being slowly covered by oil.
3. Although we tried very hard, we failed.
4. We'd rather you didn't wear those slippers in the office, Miss Blake.
5. The house had its roof blown off by the storm.
6. It's time you were able to dress yourself, Elsie.
7. There's no quicker way than this to get into the centre of the city.
8. The cause of the fire was known to only one person.
9. There is too little brandy in this punch-bowl.
10. So long as the examiners can read your handwriting, they will accept your paper.
11. In case it rains this evening, I'll take a mackintosh.
12. He had a lot of dependants.
13. His absolute frankness, more than anything else, is what I admire about him.
14. What made you think that they're rich?
15. We didn't do enough for them really.
16. I won't take up much of your time. I know you're in a hurry.
17. The older one grows, the more intolerant one becomes.
18. Only on his fourth proposal did she accept him.
19. Hardly had he arrived home when a water-heater exploded.
20. Patricia loves Mozart, but what she loves most are his operas.

31

1. misplaced
2. frozen
3. applicants
4. priceless
5. breakages
6. recipient
7. suspiciously
8. unsuitable
9. Throughout
10. beggar
11. beheaded
12. attraction
13. neighbourhood
14. outrageous
15. effortlessly
16. qualifications
17. referendum
18. childlike
19. unexpectedly
20. disconnect

32 (Suggestions only)

1 Thank you for your letter which arrived yesterday.
2 The postmark shows it was posted more than three weeks ago.
3 How bad the postal services have become recently! They are really awful!
4 Anyway, I haven't much news to tell you because everything is quiet here.
5 Except for one thing which will perhaps interest you.
6 Our daughter Jane told us yesterday that she and Ronald have decided to have their wedding at St. George's Church in a month's time.
7 They say they want a very quiet wedding so they are going to invite only a few people.
8 They haven't decided yet where they will live, but we hope it will be somewhere near us.
9 If Jane should need to come to London to buy her wedding dress, can you please put her up for the night?
10 However, I feel sure she will write to you herself to ask you if the need arises.

33

1 carrying / bringing
2 wheels
3 earth / ground / tarmac
4 back
5 wait
6 had
7 had
8 immediately / promptly
9 unable
10 alone / behind
11 spare / free / leisure
12 so
13 finished / dealt
14 made / found
15 away / gone
16 extended / renewed
17 Anything
18 approve
19 stood / endured / borne
20 though / however

34

1 it
2 one
3 them
4 herself
5 there
6 ones – ones
7 it
8 those – it
9 that
10 so
11 it / them
12 –
13 one – other
14 –
15 It

35 The red warning light appeared on the wall of the aeroplane beside the pilot's head. As I saw it, my heart gave another jump.

"Here we are, Sir," said the dispatcher cheerfully. He got up from his seat and opened the sliding door. There was a terrifying noise. The air outside seemed to be screaming furiously at us.

I felt very frightened again. I tried to calm myself by remembering what the instructor had said during the weeks of training: "No matter how often you jump you'll never lose the fear of it as you get yourself ready, but don't feel ashamed of it. It's very natural. Everybody feels afraid." I got up and approached the open doorway. I put my hands on its sides and gripped. I did not look down at the earth. I stared straight out into space, chewed on my gum, felt sick and waited, seeing the red light from the corner of my eyes.

The red light went out. The green one came on.
The dispatcher behind me said, "Ready, Sir?"
I nodded my head.
"Okay then," he said. "One – two – three – go!"

36
1 consult
2 pour
3 instructor
4 running
5 care
6 class
7 exhausting
8 apparent
9 open
10 low
11 smashed
12 shelters
13 spill
14 survived
15 attend
16 plain
17 took
18 current
19 insisted
20 watch

37
1 What would you buy if you won a lottery?
2 Won't you please turn out the light in the hall?
3 Where shall we go for our holiday this summer?
4 What is the difference between human and humane?
5 How many tins of milk do you think we should buy?
6 Why on earth didn't you telephone to say you would be so late?
7 Shall I buy this dress or that one?
8 How many people have accepted the invitation?
9 What time does the library close today?
10 Could / Can you believe that anyone can / could be so obstinate and stupid?

11 Did you dare to clean your shoes with a towel again?
12 Why does the landowner close that road once every year?
13 What sort of costume are you going to wear for the fancy-dress ball?
14 Have you seen how much washing-up has collected in the kitchen sink?
15 How long do you think I shall have to stay in bed after the operation, Doctor?

38 1 **ad**vertiser – **ad**vert**is**ement
    2 am**big**uous – am**big**uity
    3 **arch**itecture – **arch**itectural
    4 **ben**efit – **ben**eficial
    5 **cath**olic – **cath**olicism
    6 **cel**ebrate – **cel**ebrity
    7 **cer**emony – **cer**em**on**ial
    8 contri**but**ion – contri**but**ory
    9 **cour**age – **cour**ageous
    10 **dom**estic – **dom**esticity
    11 hor**iz**on – hor**iz**ontal
    12 indi**vid**ual – indi**vid**uality
    13 infor**ma**tion – infor**ma**tive
    14 man**ag**erial – **man**agement
    15 **med**icine – **med**ic**i**nal
    16 **nec**essary – **nec**ess**i**ty
    17 obli**ga**tion – obli**ga**tory
    18 pro**fess**ional – pro**fess**orial
    19 **rad**iator – **rad**iation
    20 **sol**emn – **sol**em**n**ity

39 1 had learned. learned.
    2 was charged. alleged – had been found.
    3 were. had been played – reached. were – had missed.
    4 arrived – went. found. had rained – had forgotten.
    5 came. was. had forgotten.
    6 returned – had parked – was not. thought – had been stolen – learned – had towed.
    7 had made – hoped – were – arrived.
    8 had not wanted. was – arrived. heard – had persuaded. stood. thought – was. did not speak.
    9 allowed. had hoped – had never believed. gave – told. was.
    10 found. had seen – had delayed. was – warned. decided.

40 1 b Lorna laughed with extreme nervousness.
      c Lorna's laugh was extremely nervous.
    2 b The shop assistant answered my wife with great rudeness.
      c The shop assistant's answer to my wife was very rude.

3 b The policeman did not give his evidence at the trial with complete honesty.
  c The policeman's evidence at the trial was not completely honest.
4 b The boss replied with some irony.
  b The boss's reply to me was rather ironic.
5 b Uncle Jerry lent the money with slight unwillingness.
  c Uncle Jerry's loan of the money was slightly unwilling.
6 b The medicine reacted with great unpleasantness.
  c The reaction of the medicine was most unpleasant.
7 The mechanic repaired my car with extreme inefficiency.
  The mechanic's repair of my car was extremely inefficient.
8 b I'm afraid you behaved with astonishing stupidity.
  c I'm afraid your behaviour was astonishing stupid.
9 b Aunt Fanny cut the birthday cake into eight equal pieces with great care.
  c Aunt Fanny's cutting of the birthday cake into eight equal pieces was very careful.
10 b Francis acted with complete / some absent-mindedness again.
   c Francis's action was quite absent-minded again.

41 1 The mistake is the misrelated participle: *Painted bright red, Jack always finds ...*, which means that Jack has been painted bright red. The correct version is: *His bicycle (having been) painted bright red, Jack always finds it quickly ...* or *As his bicycle is painted bright red, Jack always finds it quickly ...*
2 The mistake is the word *plenty*. Correct version: *The bus was full of people. ...* (If we want to keep the word *plenty*, we could have: *There were plenty of people on the bus ...*, but this would have a different sense.
3 The mistake is the use of the present continuous tense *are doing* with *since*. Correct version: *You have been doing this heavy digging since breakfast ...*
4 The mistake is the use of two perfect forms together: *should have liked to have gone*. The correct version is either *I should very much like to have gone* or *I should very much have liked to go*.

5 The mistake is the position of *my brother* in the relative clause. Correct version: *Those oysters that my brother ate last night.*
6 The mistake is in *I've finally got to take out all my teeth.* Correct version needs the causative construction: *I've finally got to have all my teeth taken out.*
7 The mistake is in *nobody but my father and I really enjoyed the outing.* The word *but* here means *except*, which is a preposition, and a preposition must be followed by the objective case. So the correct version is: *nobody but my father and me enjoyed the outing.*
8 The mistake is the use of *to* after *had better*. Correct version: *I think you'd better not go to school today.*
9 The mistake is the definite article *the* in front of *man*. Correct version: *In the last thirty years man has invented . . .*
10 The mistake is the past tense in the subjective 'If' – clause. Correct version: *If only they had left their house ten minutes earlier . . .*

42 1 The policeman's unwillingness to listen to the old lady's explanation made her very angry.
    2 The girl's persuasive denial that she had stolen anything made her boss believe her.
    3 My very careful obedience to your instructions brought about a perfect result.
    4 My parents' obvious dislike of my new boyfriend prevented me from inviting him home very often.
    5 Nina's impulsive purchase of a diamond necklace yesterday may cause her to abandon her holiday plans.
    6 The rapid growth of the tree was partly the result of our constant care of it.
    7 Dennis's recent loss of a leg in an accident is the reason why he has to move around in a wheelchair.
    8 My brother's fear of heights was well known to me.
    9 Jackson's disobedience of an order from an officer caused his arrest.
    10 Her belief in me encouraged me in spite of every difficulty.
    11 Our discovery of uranium on our land may make us rich.
    12 The audience's calm behaviour when the bomb went off prevented a panic and a catastrophe.
    13 That nurse's terrible carelessness cannot be excused.

14 The army's disapproval of long hair surprises very few people.
15 The Prime Minister's sharp criticism of the rebellious members of her party didn't make any difference.

43

1	round	6	off	11	through	16	by
2	after	7	through	12	round	17	into
3	into	8	off	13	over	18	by
4	after	9	with	14	through	19	with
5	with	10	off	15	over	20	into

44 (Suggestions only)

1. came again.
2. Can I help you?
3. ... forcing himself to speak with some politeness.
4. Or, perhaps I should say, good morning.
5. I just / only want ...
6. Are you so drunk that you can't see that this is a chemist's?
7. being a chemist.
8. Twenty years with no ink.
9. with a slam that might have been an explosion.
10. What were you shouting so much for?
11. everybody.
12. softly
13. What's the joke?
14. to the far end / from one end of the room to the other.
15. He climbed into bed again.
16. no matter who he is.
17. swore / cursed.
18. went
19. as quickly as possible.
20. for you, as well.

45
1. pɔːk – wɜːk
2. dɒn – wʌn
3. æs – pɑːs
4. fjvərɪ – berɪ
5. kɒst – pəvst
6. mʌŋkɪ – dɒŋkɪ
7. pɒndə(r) – wʌndə(r)
8. fɪŋgə(r) – sɪŋə(r)
9. bɪlɒŋ – əmʌŋ
10. pɑːst – gæst
11. spɪːk – breɪk
12. klɪə(r) – peə(r)
13. blʌd – gʊd
14. hɔːs – wɜːs
15. hɜːd – bɪəd
16. fɑːðə(r) – beɪðə(r)
17. sɒrɪ – wʌrɪ
18. juːθ – savθ
19. swet – hiːt
20. wɒlɪt – bæleɪ

46
1. hasn't he?
2. doesn't she?
3. had you?
4. didn't they?
5. did she?
6. aren't I?
7. didn't he?
8. is there
9. does one?
10. didn't she?
11. should you?
12. didn't they?
13. have I?
14. doesn't she?
15. was it?
16. hasn't she?
17. wouldn't she?
18. had you?
19. don't I / haven't I?
20. was he?

47
1. happened / chanced
2. retired
3. agency / office
4. bundle / bunch
5. glossy / shiny
6. brochures / pamphlets
7. over
8. enjoyed / spent
9. had
10. careful / thorough
11. varying / changing / rotating
12. showed / presented
13. average / usual / normal
14. small / minute
15. allowed / permitted
16. meals / food
17. all
18. charge / cost
19. looking
20. earlier / former / previous

48
1. We might have to buy new tyres for the car.
2. Sandra has had to break off her engagement.
3. Our parents had to leave earlier than usual.
4. This tooth will have to be taken out.
5. We used to have to sleep under mosquito nets.
6. We are sorry to announce that the Minister has had to resign from the Cabinet.
7. The landlord will certainly have to pay for this repair.

8 They were disappointed because they had had to miss our wedding.
9 The Mayor could have to abandon his plans.
10 I was sorry about the damage I caused, but I had to break the lock on the suitcase.
11 If your cheque hadn't arrived when it did, we should / would have had to ask someone to lend us some money.
12 I am going to have to lose some weight if I want to wear these trousers comfortably.
13 Since you forgot to buy bread, the whole family will have to be as economical as possible with what we have left.
14 You do not have to wait here. Please come inside.
15 Why did Gerard have to have the whole of his head shaved?

49 (*Suggestions only*)

1 stealing (line 11).
2   i pale and trembling (line 4).
   ii licked his lips (line 6).
   iii began to babble (line 10).
3 included in the affair.
4 a only just   b almost not.
5   i her narrow cunning face sharpened (line 15)
   ii sniffing danger like a vixen (line 24)
6 The danger that Mr Armroyd might permit Mr and Mrs Pentecost to stay and that they would therefore learn about what had happened.
7 a i My wife and I came in here a moment ago to settle etc.
    ii The only reason that my wife and I have come in here is to settle etc.
  b i ... to what you have as a subject.
    ii ... to what you are obliged to say.
8 He was surprised at what he had just heard.
9 He didn't want Mr Armroyd to see them.
10 Probably as evidence that might be needed later.
11 It was from the petty-cash box that Luther had been stealing (line 47).
12 Either as a success in life or to prison.
13 a A person without character or strength.
  b Make yourself seem important.
14 shaking (line 51)
15 Of Luther's guilt.

16 a Mrs Brimlow shouted that they could say what they liked, but she wouldn't believe a word of it. Their Luther was a good boy, and a hard-working boy, and a clever boy. She asked Mr Armroyd to think of / remember his own letters. Had he not written to say how good Luther was / had been, more than once.
   b Luther suddenly told his mother to leave it alone. She would do no good.
   c Mr Armroyd said that those (letters) interested him enormously. He told Mrs Brimlow that it seemed to him her son would go far – in one direction or another. Stealing from the petty-cash box was / is common enough with boys of his sort and at his age, but such a neat bit of forgery was not usual.
   d He asked Luther if he was such a poor specimen that he had to bolster himself up like that even to his own parents.
   e Mrs Brimlow shrieked at Mr Armroyd and told him to leave Luther alone. She told him he was a slave-driver and asked if it was any wonder that the poor boy stole when Mr Armroyd paid him a wage that she would be ashamed to give to a washerwoman.
17 a For a long time (line 60).
   b considerable sums of money (line 61).
   c clacking (line 63).
   d flying a bit too high (line 68).
   e He could have gone a long way (line 74).
18 occurred / come to your mind.
19 Honest and dishonest behaviour.
20 By not having him arrested at once by the police.

*The University of London School Examinations Board accepts no responsibility whatsoever for the accuracy or method of working in the answers given.

50 (*Suggestions only*)

1. I'm not going to retire until I feel like it.
2. That hotel is a bit beyond our reach, I'm afraid.
3. It doesn't matter to me whether they come or not.
4. After two hours there was still no sign of the bridegroom.
5. We didn't go to the island that stormy weekend for fear we couldn't get back.
6. Rosalind (simply) couldn't bear the heat and humidity.
7. It's going to pour. You had better take a mackintosh.
8. It was the first time many of the group had been in a helicopter.
9. Yes, I (very much) wish my father had not been so absent-minded.
10. I don't think Geoffrey will be capable of doing that job.
11. You shouldn't take so much notice of their complaints.
12. We demand to know the truth about all this.
13. Only Raymond didn't enjoy the play. / Raymond was the only one who didn't enjoy the play.
14. It's such a large house that she doesn't like being on her own in it.
15. Go and ask Winifred. She is bound to know the answer.
16. Who put you in touch with me?
17. All of a sudden, a solution to the problem occurred to Alice.
18. He is very interesting to talk to.
19. Your hair needs cutting, dear.
20. I shall never again ask you to help me.

51

1	2	3	4	5
affluent	anxious	calm	capable	deceitful
rich	frightened	peaceful	competent	deceptive
wealthy	nervous	quiet	efficient	misleading
well-to-do	timid	relaxed	experienced	untrue

52
1. post
2. daisy
3. bell
4. hunter
5. feather
6. cartload / barrowload of monkeys
7. mule
8. hills
9. mouse
10. honey
11. brave
12. clean
13. cold
14. brown
15. stiff / straight
16. pretty
17. proud
18. slippery
19. blind
20. strong

53
1. Shall we have this tree cut down?
2. Noel had his car serviced thoroughly before he started on the long journey.
3. Why didn't you have all these knives sharpened as you said you would?
4. I ought to have a light put outside the front door.
5. The Jenkinsons haven't yet had a fireplace put in their cottage as they said they would.
6. We have to have these floors polished at least once a month.
7. The law says that everyone must have seat-belts put on the front seats at least.
8. Fred doesn't have his shoes cleaned on the way to work any longer.
9. I must either buy a new typewriter or have this one repaired.
10. Let's have these curtains dyed red. They'll look much better.
11. One shouldn't forget to have the pressure of one's tyres checked from time to time.
12. My sister has had a lovely dress made out of a discarded parachute that her boyfriend gave her.
13. We had to have the car lifted on to a breakdown truck after the accident.
14. The Whittomes are having a swimming pool built in their garden.
15. Madge and Cyril didn't have enough money to have a new roof put on the house last year. They are having it put on now.

54 (*Suggestions only*)

1. Only a very brave person could have done that.
2. For fear of waking anyone up, Doris tiptoed up the stairs.
3. She said, 'You might have invited us too.'
4. Nancy prides herself on her cooking.
5. Nobody took any notice of my protests.
6. I'm sure he didn't take your umbrella deliberately / on purpose.
7. Once we arrive we'll all be able to have a beer.
8. Except for Katherine, Dolly has no real friends.
9. I wish you hadn't written that letter.
10. Nobody could find Ralph's passport.
11. We haven't been here since 1980.
12. Little does Rita realise how serious her husband's operation is going to be.
13. Rather than take it back to the shop he decided to repair the thing himself.

16. If Ivor had not helped / If it hadn't been for Ivor's help we would have been in serious trouble.
17. However experienced a driver you may be, Sir, driving at that speed on this road is dangerous.
18. Your hair really must be cut, mustn't it, Paddy?
19. It's too wonderful an opportunity for us to miss.
20. Paul didn't say a word as he left the room.

55

1. c
2. b
3. a
4. b
5. c
6. a
7. b
8. b
9. c
10. a

56
1. destruction
2. employer – employees
3. encouragement
4. sleepy
5. carriage
6. truthful
7. ashamed
8. organisation
9. worthless
10. disobedience
11. apologetic
12. colonisation
13. unfavourable
14. heady
15. imperfect
16. worn-out
17. strengthening
18. thefts
19. generosity
20. devaluation

57 (*Suggestions only*)

1. I am at present a student in my final year at the City High School in Harare, Zimbabwe.
2. I have been studying English for five years now.
3. In June this year I shall be sitting for the First Certificate examination of the University of Cambridge, and I hope to pass with a good grade.
4. I also expect to obtain the High School Certificate at about the same time with high marks, particularly in biology.
5. My ambition is to enter London University in due course and to read for a degree in genetics.
6. I realise it is necessary to have the G.C.E. to qualify for entrance to the university.
7. I very much hope I will be accepted by your College in order to prepare for the G.C.E. in Chemistry and Biology, and in English too.
8. I would like to start in the early autumn so as not to waste time.
9. Perhaps I should add that my father and mother are both doctors, so I have been brought up in a scientific environment.
10. I would be most grateful if you would send me your official application form and inform me about what other information about myself is required.

58
1. mood / temper / humour
2. approached
3. matter / trouble / problem
4. couple / number
5. like
6. for
7. used / accustomed / hardened
8. grant / give
9. comprehension / understanding
10. put
11. sooner / quicker
12. away / home / out
13. head
14. upset / annoyed / irritated / angered
15. just
16. was
17. finally / eventually
18. done
19. Amid / In / After
20. suit / become

59
1. bought
2. has lived / has been living
3. have lost
4. washed
5. comes
6. went
7. should / would have been
8. arrives
9. have seen
10. were
11. haven't had
12. has been looking / (has looked★)
13. had known
14. were having / (had had★)
15. shall / will have been
16. has been invited
17. had been working / (had worked★)
18. arrives
19. were coming / would come / could come
20. has forgotten

(★ possible, but not so logical)

60
1. to the point
2. from time to time
3. in time
4. on the point
5. At times
6. against time
7. in point
8. By the time
9. in time
10. beside the point
11. at the same time
12. at one time
13. up to a point
14. to the point
15. on time

177

61
1. a collector of stamps
2. a head with the shape of an egg
3. The story of his life
4. reviews of films
5. steps of solid marble
6. the sonnets of Shakespeare
7. the noise of aircraft
8. the Secretary of the Club
9. a member of a union
10. a lecture of one-and-a-half-hours
11. (the) owners of helicopters
12. Lovers of music
13. The obstinacy of a mule
14. an expensive mackintosh of rubberised-silk
15. the lifting of weights
16. a wall of cardboard
17. a bracelet of eighteen-carat gold
18. the light of a candle
19. a / the cover of a book
20. The making of roads

62
1. scatter
2. got over
3. advantage
4. permit
5. reliable
6. recovered
7. tripped
8. eccentric
9. precautions
10. staple
11. trend
12. abstained
13. ingredients
14. condition
15. diverted
16. illegible
17. evaluated
18. obstacle
19. ingenious
20. capacity

63
1. bʌrə
2. bʌv
3. kɒf
4. dəv
5. hɪkʌp
6. plʌv
7. rʌf
8. θʌrə
9. ðəv
10. θruː
11. tʌf
12. trɒf

64
1. have forgotten.
2. came – was – has become.
3. has not arrived – has not telephoned – said.
4. has (ever) had.
5. took – took – have looked – have been put.
6. has appeared – bought.
7. have come — have asked – have all said / said.
8. was – were – gave – said – was not.
9. have finished – did not expect.
10. started – have not finished.
11. went – was – wasted – Have (any of you) seen.
12. asked / have asked – have not received.

13 has been.
14 was – sold – went – has (already) sold
15 escaped – has been captured – shot – made – wounded – was captured – used – was brought.

65

1	2	3	4	5
attach	bang	beat	liberate	march
fasten	knock	cane	ransom	stroll
fix	rap	spank	rescue	tramp
secure	tap	thrash	save	wander

66 (*Suggestions only*)

1 you had been / come
2 have been looking
3 you keep / go
4 action / steps would you have
5 has been
6 better tell
7 neither does / nor does
8 -room / -bedroom
9 would stop / wouldn't go on
10 shall we
11 you haven't given
12 amount of
13 one of the nicest people
14 will be your own
15 your hands up in the
16 we had not
17 will have to be done
18 could have gone to the
19 have been doing / going
20 to going to / to being sent to

67

1 must	4 must	7 might	10 would	13 might
2 might	5 can	8 must	11 can	14 would
3 would	6 might	9 can	12 must	15 can

179

68 (*Suggestions only*)

1. Have all of you understood all that?
2. Didn't anyone inform you that there is going to be a meeting?
3. We (I / She / They etc.) had to throw the chair away because someone had broken its springs.
4. My father wants to resign but the company has asked him to stay on for another year or so. They say his presence on the Board is valuable.
5. Did the Queen herself give the medal?
6. They are going to build a new stretch of motorway between Graz and Lund.
7. Many ambitious men see politics as a stepping-stone to power.
8. Thieves had smashed a window and stolen everything that was in the car.
9. People often confuse the meanings of these two words.
10. Do all their policemen wear those funny hats?
11. Some people wrongly believe that antibiotics are the cure for a common cold.
12. Who wrote this? I insist on your telling me the truth.
13. At last they have invited us to one of their receptions.
14. We (They, etc.) are turning the one-time storeroom above the garage into a spare bedroom.
15. They allow you to go there only if you are a Moslem.
16. A small box which someone had placed under the Minister's car suddenly caught the policeman's attention.
17. The manager summoned Maurice, strongly reprimanded him, and threatened him with immediate dismissal if he ever did the same thing again.
18. The burning question that faces this Government is what it can do about unemployment.
19. During the month that the terrorists held the General prisoner, they chained him to his bed for twenty-three-and-a-half hours out of twenty-four. And they did not ever allow / let him see their faces or hear their voices.
20. Very well, Sir. We shall give your car our 'B' Service this morning. We shall wash and polish it this afternoon, and return it to you at five o'clock.

69
1. out
2. off
3. through
4. outs
5. in
6. down
7. by – down
8. overs
9. up
10. up
11. between
12. up
13. off
14. over
15. out

70
1. en*tirely* en*vel*oped
2. ex*tremely* eligible bach*el*or
3. re*cord* dis*cuss*ion
4. un*fort*unately *ref*use can*al*
5. ex*pand* con*tract*
6. *ir*ritating *up*sets
7. corres*pond*ents sub*ject*ed *front*ier
8. *con*tract mi*nute*
9. *ex*tract *in*juries
10. ex*ec*utive ad*min*istrative responsi*bil*ities.

71 (*Suggestions only*)
1. Because a) shops are closed over Christmas and b) servants (if they exist) must have some time free.
2. finally
3. From excitement and (possibly) from a reflection of a light.
4. It has a different meaning. It emphasises the sense of *even with the toys too.*
5. Both are operated by the same sort of mechanism.
6. Because it does not mean 'Honestly, it's too early.' It prefaces a separate thought; for example: 'Honestly, these children of mine!'
7. 'Oh, all right. Come and get warm, you little goat.'
8. The plan of the children to wake their parents up much earlier than they would want to be woken up.
9. Because their excuses (lines 20 and 26) were so obviously false.
10. Because, until now, they had been trying to pretend it had not yet begun, because it was still so early in the morning.
11. He was too young to have fully developed fingers.
12. He liked it more than the other toys, so he separated it.
13. Yes. It means that we do not always manage to have what we want in life, even though that thing seems to be within our reach.
14. anxiety.

15 She knew that Toby took after her in an attitude to life, but she knew that 'the ball sometimes rolled away'. She was therefore anxious on his behalf.

16 a In line 6 it means *sufficiently*; in line 42 it means *quite* or *rather*.
   b In line 19 it means *so early as to be unacceptable*; in line 22 it means *as well*.
   c In line 20 it expresses strong supposition; in line 22 it expresses necessity.

17 Most thoughtful: Toby. (... *he arranged them in a neat pattern on the bed-cover and looked at them in complete silence for a long time* (lines 38–40)).
   Most impulsive: Judy (... *pulled all her treasures out in a heap, took a quick glance at them and went straight for the one she liked best* (lines 36–37)).

18 a had been completely successful.
   b Nothing else could be done.
   c immediately selected.
   d almost without intending to, he would look at the ball.
   e giving the impression that he wanted to be certain that it was still there.

19 a doing up (line 2).   d by itself (line 41).
   b on purpose (line 7).   e from time to time (line 42).
   c barefoot (line 12).

20 a complained   g obvious
   b putting up   h pliable
   c arranging   i inspected
   d noisily   j orderly
   e be regarded   k total
   f tightly holding   l wander

72 (Suggestions only)

1. It's to wash (ourselves) in.
2. It's to do sums with.
3. It's to take photographs with.
4. It's to keep a prisoner in.
5. It's to light a fire in.
6. It's to make electricity with.
7. They're to cover your hands with.
8. They're to dress a wound with.
9. It's to wash-up in.
10. It's to take notes in.
11. It's to jump from an aeroplane in / with.
12. It's to wander or relax in.
13. It's to shave with.
14. It's to be educated at.
15. They're to cut things with.
16. It's to kill birds or game with.
17. It's to eat or sit at.
18. It's to get a degree at.
19. It's to record TV programmes on.
20. It's to play music on.

73

1. I wish I had gone on the earlier train.
2. I wish Rolls-Royces were not so expensive.
3. I wish I hadn't bought these shoes.
4. I wish you didn't persist in doing these stupid things.
5. I wish Aunt Victoria were coming to our party.
6. I wish you didn't waste your time so foolishly.
7. I wish I hadn't had to bring the plumber for such a small job. I wish I had been able to do/could have done it myself.
8. Clive wishes he had taken the opportunity that we offered him.
9. I wish your mother were not such an interfering woman. I wish she would stop meddling in our affairs.
10. ... I wish I had not had that last drink at their party.
11. Father wishes he did not have to get up so early tomorrow.
12. Brian says he wishes he could have done/had been able to do what you asked him.

13 If Evelyn hadn't stayed on late to finish the job, he would have wished he had.

14 ... I wish you were more careful.

15 I wish we could find a taxi.

16 I wish we could have got/had been able to get seats for something last summer at the Salzburg Festival.

17 The manager later said he wished he had not left before we arrived at his office.

18 I wish we had chosen a slightly less expensive hotel to stay at.

19 ... and now she wishes she had.

20 I wish you didn't have to be asked to resign your membership of this club.

74
1 appears / seems
2 poorly / barely
3 Barely / Scarcely / Hardly
4 articles / items / pieces
5 appear
6 wills / testaments
7 mention
8 worthy
9 naturally
10 roughly / crudely / rudely
11 intended / meant / supposed
12 up
13 thought
14 when / if
15 whole / entire
16 share
17 until / to
18 left / bequeathed
19 heightened / increased
20 practice / habit / custom

75
1 Do you mind my sitting here for a few minutes?
2 I'm going to put you in charge of today's programme.
3 Everybody is going to be given a raise / rise.
4 Did Pamela give any reason for being so late?

5 You needn't have done all that washing-up.
6 Things are always going wrong in a job of this sort.
7 The agent described it as a magnificent, eighteenth-century mansion.
8 We were on the point of going to bed when the earthquake happened.
9 Tony bought Stella a necklace to make up for not having a holiday.
10 The doctor says that Stanley's liver will be all right now, provided he doesn't start drinking again.
11 The stories he tells about his war experiences are beyond belief.
12 I spend an awful lot on (running) my car these days.
13 It's a month now since she fell down the stairs but the bruises still show.
14 There is no room in the garden for a swimming pool to be built.
15 How fast is one allowed to go on this motorway?
16 They might be millionaires, the way they live!
17 It was near enough for us to walk / have walked to the station.
18 Don't bother to telephone me when you arrive.
19 Should one really freeze this sort of food?
20 I wasn't allowed to go into the hospital to see the survivors.

76

1	2	3	4	5
associate	command	fear	irony	lane
colleague	direction	fright	mockery	path
mate	order	panic	ridicule	track
partner	regulation	terror	sarcasm	way

77
1. sandboy
2. rock
3. pig
4. falling off a log
5. vinegar
6. nails
7. sin
8. sheet
9. bone
10. lobster
11. quick
12. bright
13. sober
14. soft
15. cool
16. dead
17. good
18. pure
19. pale
20. black

78
1. some – any – ones – ones
2. Some – any
3. one – ones
4. some – some – some – Any
5. any – some
6. Any – one
7. any – some – any – some
8. any – ones – some – some
9. some
10. some – any – any

79 (*Suggestions only*)
1. You like this food more than I (do).
2. I was particularly impressed by her accent-free pronunciation.
3. At no time was the result of the match in doubt.
4. This will be the first time the orchestra has performed outside London.
5. When did this roof begin leaking? / start to leak?
6. Lydia had some soup spilled over her new dress (by a waiter) last night.
7. My family hasn't written to me recently.
8. You can't have enjoyed that party very much, can you?

9 If I hadn't had my cheque-book on me, we would have been in trouble.
10 You'd better go and ask her yourself.
11 There was no justification for the violent criticism of the Prime Minister.
12 Who does that car outside the gate belong to?
13 Unless it rains soon, a lot of our crops will be lost.
14 We'll still go even if it rains.
15 There's nothing I wouldn't do for him.
16 Veronica didn't forget, and neither did Dorothy.
17 What reaction would you have had?
18 Aren't we ever going to be brought the breakfast I ordered for 8 o'clock?
19 Nobody who was there can remember anything unusual happening.
20 It was because I refused to obey the policeman that I was arrested.

80 (*Suggestions only*)

1 I was so glad to get your letter and learn that you'll be able to come and spend part of your summer holiday here.
2 I doubt whether our weather will be so good as it is in Greece but I hope it won't be too bad.
3 The sea is not more than fifteen minutes away from my house so perhaps some bathing will be possible.
4 At first you will find our sea cold – particularly since you are accustomed to the Mediterranean – but you'll soon get used to it.
5 Unfortunately I can't manage to come to London to meet you, but if you're able to get the train to Brighton I will meet you at the station.
6 It's only an hour's journey by train from London to Brighton, from Victoria Station.

7   It has become easier and quicker to reach Victoria Station.

8   Simply take the airport bus, which now goes direct to Grosvenor Gardens, opposite the station.

9   When you get to Victoria, telephone me to tell me your arrival time in Brighton. You already have my number in my last letter to you.

10 When you reach Brighton I expect you will recognise me from my photograph but I will be wearing or carrying (depending on the weather) a light-grey raincoat to make extra sure.

81
1   handful
2   satisfactory
3   accuracy
4   hindrance
5   reproduction
6   anxiety
7   comparatively
8   independent
9   pointless
10 impoliteness
11 straightening
12 unreliable
13 selfishness
14 inexperienced
15 orphanage
16 rightful
17 scarcity
18 severity
19 trustworthy
20 security

82
1   ... There is no hot water left.
2   ... we saw nobody we knew very well.
3   You can find nothing like this outside Austria.
4   There are no more eggs in the refrigerator.
5   We went nowhere else that weekend.
6   They decided to do no more work that day.
7   ... but I have none to spare.
8   I'm sorry to say I think he has none at all.
9   The baker has closed and we have no bread. . . . except for the fact that we have none of that either.
10 ... There's nothing on TV worth staying up for.

83
1. It
2. with
3. put / laid
4. if / though
5. far
6. took
7. marking / noting / keeping
8. shook
9. mean / intend / want / wish
10. regarded / studied
11. far
12. Well / So
13. time / days
14. just / simply / merely / only
15. There
16. Nobody / No one
17. did
18. searched / examined
19. wonder / doubt
20. right / correct

84
1. on end
2. at full tilt
3. in the end
4. to the full
5. no end
6. at full blast
7. at the end
8. in full swing
9. at an end
10. full length
11. By the end
12. in full bloom
13. to the end
14. in full
15. on the end

85
1. What have you forgotten?
2. Whose address have you forgotten?
3. Where are you going next month?
4. What part of France are you going to next month?
5. When are you going to the south of France?
6. Which month are you going to the south of France?
7. What was their house struck by again last night?
8. What happened to their house again last night?
9. What do they say doesn't strike twice in the same place?
10. How far is it from Salzburg to Vienna?

11 How many kilometres is it from Salzburg to Vienna?
12 From where to Vienna is it about 300 kilometres?
13 From Salzburg to where is it about 300 kilometres?
14 What is the thing that Mildred wants most?
15 Who is the one who wants a quiet house in the country?
16 What sort of house in the country does Mildred want most?
17 What sort of tablets does Conrad have to take twice a day to build up his strength?
18 How often does Conrad have to take vitamin tablets to build up his strength?
19 How many times a day does Conrad have to take vitamin tablets to build up his strength?
20 Why does Conrad have to take vitamin tablets twice a day?

86
1 get over
2 get back
3 get away
4 get out of
5 getting on
6 took you for
7 takes after
8 takes back
9 take her out
10 take over
11 make out
12 made for
13 make up for
14 made off with
15 make – out of it

87
1 murdered
2 mild
3 compulsive
4 queue
5 lack
6 outbreak
7 see through
8 work out
9 put across
10 otherwise
11 fallen out
12 value
13 called off
14 cross
15 cross
16 plain
17 showing off
18 take in
19 view
20 pieces

88 a (*Seafood*) anchovy, carp, catfish, clam, cod, crab, crayfish, dogfish, eel, haddock, halibut, herring, lobster, lungfish, mullet, mussel, octopus, oyster, pike, plaice, prawn, roach, salmon, sardine, scallop, shark, shrimp, skate, sole, squid, trout, whiting.

b (*Meat*) beef, boar, chicken, duck, goose, grouse, hare, lamb, mutton, partridge, pheasant, pork, quail, rabbit, snail, turkey, veal, venison, woodcock.

c (*Vegetable*) artichoke, asparagus, aubergine (US: eggplant), bean, beetroot, Brussels sprout, carrot, cassava, cauliflower, celery, cucumber, gherkin, green pepper, leek, lentil, lettuce, marrow, okra, onion, pea, potato, pumpkin, radish, soybean, spinach, spring onion (US: scallion), tomato, turnip, yam.

d (*Fruit*) apple, apricot, avocado, banana, blackberry, blackcurrant, cherry, coconut, cranberry, cumquat, date, elderberry, fig, gooseberry, grape, kiwi fruit, lemon, loquat, lychee, mango, melon, olive, orange, papaya, peach, pear, pineapple, plum, pomegranate, raspberry, redcurrant, strawberry, tangerine.

89
1 a
2 –
3 the
4 a
5 the / an
6 –
7 a
8 –
9 a
10 a
11 a
12 –
13 the
14 a
15 a
23 the
24 the / a
25 the
26 the
27 the
28 –
29 a
30 the
31 the / a
32 the
33 –
34 a
35 –
36 a
37 a
44 –
45 the
46 –
47 The
48 the
49 the
50 The
51 the
52 the
53 the
54 – / the
55 – / the
56 – / the
57 the
58 the
65 a
66 an
67 a / the
68 the
69 A
70 – / the
71 the
72 the
73 –
74 –
75 the
76 – / the
77 –
78 –
79 the

16	a	38	the	59	A	80	the
17	–	39	–	60	the	81	–
18	a	40	the	61	–	82	the
19	a	41	–	62	–/the	83	–
20	the	42	–/the	63	–/the	84	the
21	–	43	the	64	the	85	the/a
22	the						

90 (*Suggestions only*)

1 We have placed the money to the credit of your current account at this bank.
2 Montague was busy putting oil on his shotgun.
3 The road to the farm has at last been covered with asphalt.
4 They are going to make a film about the story of her life.
5 My wife is very fond of working in the garden.
6 Enemy planes dropped bombs on the centre of the city.
7 I want to make a reservation of two seats for this evening's performance.
8 Your name is at the head of the list of successful applicants.
9 Cynthia worked as a nurse for two years in this hospital before she got married.
10 As the police approached, the demonstrators threw stones at them.
11 Aunt Florence spent the morning taking weeds out of the lawn.
12 Waiter, may we give our order now, please?
13 Since my accident, I have been finding it difficult to tie the laces of my shoes.
14 The policeman was so unhelpful that my aunt just couldn't keep her temper under control.
15 ... I have only written it in pencil on these papers.

91
1. were not used to
2. use
3. used to
4. use
5. haven't used
6. are used to
7. to be used
8. haven't used
9. became / grew used to
10. used to
11. using
12. not to use
13. have used / have been using
14. was used to – to get / become / grow used to
15. used to – use

92 (*Suggestions only*)

1. bull: 'He tells a lot of *cock and bull* stories about his war experiences.'
2. dried: 'The situation changes so fast,' said the industry spokesman, 'that we would all be masterminds if we had our policy *cut and dried*.'
3. blood: 'I just can't do any more work today. I'm only *flesh and blood*!'
4. chattels: 'The removal van will take the furniture to the new flat, but we can take most of the *goods and chattels* in the car.'
5. fast: 'I'm afraid there's no *hard and fast* rule about that piece of grammar.'
6. shoulders: 'That hotel is *head and shoulders* above the others in the place.'
7. seek: 'The children are playing *hide and seek* in the woods.'
8. mighty: 'My brother-in-law has become very *high and mighty* since he was elected to Parliament.'
(**Note:** *dry* is also possible: 'The tour company went bankrupt and left many of its customers *high and dry* in foreign countries.')
9. ends: 'Children, it's time for bed. But put away all these *odds and ends* first.'

10 proper: 'I think Agatha is a bit too *prim and proper* to approve of that sort of joke.'

11 cons: 'They didn't weigh up the *pros and cons* of the matter before they made their decision.'

12 tired: 'I'm getting *sick and tired* of your constant grumbling.'

13 span: 'The two sisters are so unlike in their ways. Mary's room always looks like a battleground, while Joan's is always *spick and span*.'

14 nail: 'I'm not surprised they've separated. They've been fighting *tooth and nail* for years now.'

15 tear: 'The furniture suffers a lot of *wear and tear* when the children are at home.'

93 (*Suggestions only*)

1 No, I didn't forget to give her your message.
2 Many people consider Brown's Hotel (to be) one of the best in London.
3 It was such mild weather that we didn't need coats.
4 Winston denies having (had) anything to do with the matter.
5 Virginia learned to ski at the age of five.
6 I had only three hours' sleep last night.
7 I did not telephone you as promised because my brother suddenly arrived.
8 There's no point in trying to mend this tyre.
9 I'm going to let you off this time.
10 Christine came into a large fortune on her father's death.
11 Only Timothy didn't think the hotel was worth its high prices.
12 His second book is much less interesting than his first.
13 Where would you rather go tonight? The theatre or the cinema?

14 The murderer wiped the gun in case his fingerprints should give him away.

15 It's going to cost an awful lot.

16 Who is to blame for all this mess?

17 The difference between us is that I don't have to retire when I'm sixty.

18 That house is worth looking at again.

19 We look upon it as a wonderful opportunity.

20 There is hardly anything in the house to eat tonight.

94 1 cross-question: to question someone very closely (i.e. in a court of law) in order to compare the answers with other answers given before.
crossword: a game in which words are fitted into a pattern of numbered squares.

2 fruit fly: any of several types of small fly that feed on fruit.
fruit machine: a machine with a long handle, into which people put money in order to win more money.

3 gaslight: the light produced from burning gas.
gas-mask: a breathing apparatus worn over the face to protect the wearer from poisonous gases.

4 girlfriend: a girl or woman with whom a boy or man spends time and shares amusements.
girlhood: the state or time of being a young girl.

5 highland: a mountainous area.
high tea: an early evening meal taken instead of afternoon tea and dinner, and at a time between the times of those meals.

6 mouth-organ: a type of small musical instrument, played by being held to the mouth and blown into or sucked.
   mouthpiece: i the part of anything that is held in or near the mouth;
   ii a person or newspaper etc. that expresses the opinions of others;
   iii (American) a lawyer who defends people charged with crimes.

7 oil-cloth: cloth treated with oil so that water will not go through it, used for covering tables, shelves, etc.
   oilfield: an area of land under which there is oil.

8 postmark: an official mark made on letters etc., usually over the stamp, showing when and from where they are sent.
   postscript: a short addition to a letter, below the place where one has signed one's name.

9 roundabout: i a central space at a road crossing, which makes cars go in a circle round it and not straight across.
   ii a machine in an amusement park on which children can ride round and round sitting on wooden animals.
   round trip: a journey to a place and back again.

10 sunstroke: an illness with fever, weakness and headache caused by the effects of too much strong sunlight, especially on the head.
    suntan: the brownness of the skin after exposure to the sun.

11 Sunday best: very good clothes which are worn only on special occasions, especially (originally) for church.
    Sunday school: a place or occasion for giving children religious teaching on a Sunday.

12 test case: a case in a court of law which establishes a particular principle and is then used as a standard against which other cases can be judged.
test tube: a small tube of thin glass, closed at one end, used in scientific tests.

13 toothache: a pain in a tooth.
toothpick: a short, thin, pointed piece of wood used for removing food stuck between the teeth.

14 whip hand: the possession of power or control over somebody.
whip-round: a collection of money among a group of people, as in a place of work, to buy something for one member.

15 workroom: a room which is specially kept for working in.
workshop: a room or place, as in a factory, where heavy repairs and jobs on machines are done.

95 1 acknowledged / admitted

2 hardly / barely / scarcely

3 gaze / look

4 infants / offspring

5 So-and-so / What's-his-name

6 should / can

7 racks

8 hardly likes / does not want

9 what sex it is / about its sex

10 is saved / may be saved

11 screaming / protesting / screeching

12 does not have to / need not

13 Then / There

14 banging / hitting / knocking

15 speak

16 In the end / Finally

17 in case / for fear

18 To

19 a matter / a question

20 altogether / entirely / completely

96
1 up	4 on	7 down	10 out	13 out
2 by	5 by	8 over	11 in	14 up
3 out	6 in	9 over	12 down	15 up

97 (*Suggestions only*)

1 Mr Phanourakis was eighty-five years of age when he left his Greek mountain village for ever.

2 His sons had been successful in the restaurant business there.

3 The old gentleman did not know any other language but Greek.

4 He found his way around the foreign ship without difficulty.

5 The majority of the others waited for the chief steward to tell them which were their tables.

6 A few moments later his table companion arrived and sat down in the other chair.

7 One of the ship's officers, who knew some Greek, asked the old gentleman if he had found anyone he knew on the ship.

8 'I suppose he is French. His name is Bonapetit – or something of that sort.'

9 'I was foolish not to understand.'

10 The Frenchman smiled back at him.

98 (*Suggestions only*)

1. Because the church is in the way.
2. Because there is a nice view of Steen Lake, if one has a room overlooking it.
3. By going through the tunnel that is under the railway line.
4. 'Go along this street and take the second turning to the left. You'll find the Princess Hotel on the left (facing the lake) a little more than half way along that street.'
5. In the Market Square opposite the Town Hall.
6. I would go forward across the side of the square until I reached Burton Street on my left. I would go along Burton Street, through the tunnel, as far as Taylor Road at its far end. I would then turn right, and find Mr Brent's house a little way along on the right.
7. At the corner of Charles Street and St Peter's Lane.
8. Because, instead of going straight over the railway line to Hare Street, I would have to go a long way round by Taylor Road and Burton Street and Maxwell Street.
9. Because it leads to London.
10. Along the River Steen into Steen Lake or down river towards London.

99

1. scarcely
2. rarely
3. even
4. still
5. yet
6. already
7. never
8. Scarcely
9. frequently
10. still – even
11. yet
12. already
13. still
14. scarcely
15. Even

100 (*Suggestions only*)

1. Probably because she realised that her answer was not a good one.
2. Perhaps to hold their attention until he got to the interesting part.
3. To compensate for all the dull good points about the girl.
4. Because, to them, such goodness was horrible.
5. Because the bachelor had been faced with his first 'Why?'.
6. That he had a very quick imagination. *calmly* (line 61); *promptly* (line 74).
7. The bachelor's answer was not only quickly given, it was also clever.
8. She disapproved of the conversation about dirtiness.
9. Because she would not have the pleasure of knowing she had kept her promise.
10. I have never heard such a stupid story.
11. Because there is no emphasis on the number. The words *a third* simply mean *another*.
12. For that reason a sheep was never kept by the Prince in his park or a clock in his palace.
13. Did a sheep or a clock kill the Prince?
14. *annoyed at* – irritated by.   *quite* – rather.
    whatever – anything.   *extra* – specially.
    trace – indication.   *meant* – intended.
15. Because the wolf meant danger, and danger meant excitement.
16. From anticipation of excitement. To provide the excitement.
17. No. He was probably hoping she would be in danger.
18. They probably couldn't believe their ears.
19. They were very happy about what had happened to Bertha.

20   They hardly dared to believe that a story could have such an ending.

21   Probably because of his success as a story-teller. By letting goodness have a disastrous result.

22   a   'You don't seem much of a success as a story-teller.' (line 11)
     b   'I kept them quiet for ten minutes, which was more than you were able to do.' (line 129)
     He may have been irritated by the way the aunt handled the children, and perhaps by the stupidity of her story.

23   The bigger girl asked whether any of the little pigs had been killed.
   The bachelor told her that they had not. They had all escaped.
   There was another pause.
   The smaller of the girls said that the story had begun very badly, but it had had a very beautiful ending.
   The bigger of the girls said it was the most beautiful story she had ever heard.
   Cyril said it was the *only* beautiful story he had ever heard.
   The aunt began to splutter, and exclaimed that it had been a most improper story to tell to young children. She asked him how he had dared. He had destroyed the effect of years of careful teaching.
   The train began to slow down.
   The bachelor, standing up and collecting his things, said that at any rate he had kept them quiet for ten minutes, which was more than she had been able to do.
   Cyril asked him not to go, but to tell them another story.

24   a   discover by smelling (where Bertha was).
     b   there was no reason for him not to go off.
     c   was on the point of moving away / was ready to move away.
     d   The aunt began to speak in a confused and angry way.

25   *awakening* – return   *gleaming* – shining
     spotlessly – perfectly   *ferocity* – fierceness

INDEX

** These exercises are modelled on questions that appear regularly in the Cambridge First Certificate examination.

* These exercises are modelled on other questions that have appeared in recent years in the same examination.

All references are to exercise numbers not to page numbers.

COMPREHENSION AND APPRECIATION   21, 49, 71, 100

GRAMMAR

A (an), the, or no article?   *89
Active to passive   14
Difference of meaning in pairs of sentences?   18
Find mistake in sentences   41
Find suitable preposition or particle   *22
Find suitable tense   *59
Form question tags   46
Form questions   85
Have for causation   53
Have to for *necessary*   48
No one, nothing, none. Which?   82
Omission of *each other, yourself*, etc.   9
Passive to active   68
Past simple and past perfect tenses   39
Past simple and present perfect tenses   64
Rearrange order of words   37
Rephrase with the verb *wish*   73
Reported speech   23
Some, any, one, ones. Which?   78

Use, used to, get used to *91
Which phrase suitably fills blank space? 17

PRONUNCIATION 13, 20, 45, 63

REPHRASING

Combine pairs of sentences *42
Complete unfinished letters **7, 32, 57, 80
Complete unfinished sentences **5, 30, 54, 79
Fill blank spaces with suitable word or phrase 16, 66
Omit certain words or phrases, and rephrase 28, 34, 44, 97
Rephrase sentences using given word 6, 25, 50, 75, 93
Rephrase using *too* or *enough* 26
Rephrase with nouns and adjectives 40
Substitute noun phrases 90
Use phrases with **of** 61

STRESS 10, 38, 70

VOCABULARY

Acceptance/accusation/admission, etc. Which? *4
as mad as a . . . ., as deaf as a . . ., etc. 52, 77
ask/speak/tell/talk etc. Which? *2
Choose suitable modal *67
Complete pairs: *bits & . . . ., odds & . . . .*, etc. 92
Find particle for phrasal verbs *19, 43, 69, 86, 96
Find suitable word for blank spaces in passage **8, 33, 58, 83
in hand/at hand, at times/in time, etc. *12, 60, 84
Names of the things we eat 88
Notice/noticeable, Receive/reception, etc. *6, 31, 56, 81
Rarely/scarcely/yet/never, etc. Which? 99
Rearrange adjectives/verbs/nouns in groups 51, 65, 76
Which of four words suitably fills blanks space **11, 36, 62, 87
Which of three words could fill spaces in passage? 24, 47, 74, 95
Which things are associated with which people? 27
Which word describes certain things? *3, 15
Which words form standard compounds? 94

MISCELLANEOUS

B.B.C./C.I.A./Y.M.C.A., etc. Meanings? 29
Meanings of idiomatic expressions 55
Punctuation 35
Questions from a map 98
Telephone conversation: what did the other say? 1
What's a . . . for? 72

203